English Un

1852 –2012

From Freedom to Control

Michael Baatz

First published in Great Britain 2013

Published by Downland Publishing Sherborne
Downland House 4 Gainsborough Drive
Sherborne Dorset DT9 6DR
U.K Tel: +44 (0)1935 814977

ISBN: 978-0-9576210-0-8

Printed and bound by
Shelleys The Printers Ltd
Western Ways Yard
Bristol Road Sherborne

Contents

ENGLISH UNIVERSITIES 1852–1992 PART 1
FROM FREEDOM TO DIRECTION

English universities (except for the University of Buckingham) get most of their income from central government. Up to 1960 each was founded by personal or civic initiatives and funded privately and locally. For a hundred years they operated as virtually free agents. Today they remain legally independent and self-governing with a uniquely democratic management structure but they are subject to such Central Government direction that they appear to be part of a 'National Service' of higher education. This paper traces their passage over 160 years from independence to direction and control. It has three parts – first the foundations; second early government funding; and lastly political perspectives. For the history of the early period I am indebted to Sir James Mountford's "British Universities"(OUP 1966), Wikipedia and university web-sites.

Private endowments and initiatives founded many Oxbridge colleges and most 'redbrick' universities of the 19th century. Civic or community initiatives founded London and some others. (ANNEX 1). In Manchester manufacturer and merchant John Owens (1790-1846) left £96,000 in his will to endow a college which opened in March 1851 as Owens College. In Southampton in 1850 H.R. Hartley, son of a prosperous wine merchant, bequeathed £102,000 to the Corporation of Southampton for "the study and advancement of the sciences, natural history, and classical learning". The Hartley Institute was opened in 1862 with the money remaining after lawsuits disputing the will. In Leeds in 1872 an engineer James Kitson fostered a scheme for a college of science and in 1874 the Yorkshire College of Science was opened providing instruction in sciences and arts applicable to the industries of the county of Yorkshire. In Sheffield wealthy steel manufacturer Mark Firth (1819-1880) provided a site, a building and an endowment for a college of Arts and Science which opened in 1879. In Birmingham Sir Josiah Mason (1795-1881), who left school aged eight, gave £200,000 to found a college which opened in 1880 as the Mason Science College. Civic pride and civic financial support gave birth to other foundations. In Bristol the Society of Merchant Venturers supported the foundation of a university college and in 1876 the college was incorporated. A medical school in the town established in 1833 became part of the college in 1893. In Liverpool the city provided a site and premises and an endowment fund and its college opened in 1882. In Nottingham an anonymous donor offered £10,000 for a building to house the mechanics institute and natural history museum and the town found the balance of funds required for the new institution which opened in 1881. In Reading the history was somewhat different. Schools of Art and Science were established in Reading in 1860 and 1870 and in 1892 these Schools were transferred by the Town Council to the "College at Reading" which was founded that year by Christ Church College Oxford as an extension college. The college received its first treasury grant in 1901and in 1904 it was given a site by the Palmer family who supported opening of Wantage Hall in 1908 and of the Research Institute in Dairying in 1912. In Exeter in 1865 the city had erected a building, as a memorial to the Prince Consort, to house its art school and county museum and in 1893 this was designated as the Exeter Technical and University Extension College.

For these higher education colleges the early years were challenging. Yet none failed for three main reasons. First each had the support of a group of lay people who regarded its success as a personal challenge. They worked for the college in maintaining public interest and fund-raising and discussed with the academic staff the needs of the college and how to meet them. Second were the professors and lecturers who joined the new institutions and were determined that the college would succeed and would in time be a full university. Third was the London University which under its 1836 and 1839 Charters set examinations for award of degrees but did not concern itself with how "external" students prepared for its examinations whether by private study, correspondence courses or attending courses at a local college. The University set the syllabuses for each degree, set the examination papers and appointed the examiners. So the newly established "University Colleges" could teach for the London examinations and later announce in their Prospectuses that "The College offers courses for the External Degrees of the University of London in Arts, Science, Commerce, Economics and Law." The position was not ideal for the teaching staff of the Colleges. They did not define their own syllabuses, nor set the examinations nor mark them. But they were teaching clearly at the level of the University of London and could claim academic parity with other universities.

Finance was a continuing anxiety to the colleges though some had continuing patrons. The Wills family, for example, were large benefactors to Bristol, the Boot family to Nottingham and the Palmer family to Reading. But, for most, funds were severely limited. After the initial enthusiasm it proved less easy to obtain donations, bequests were naturally delayed, and local government became concerned about increasing grants from the rates.

Government regular funding of the universities as a group began in 1889 when Central Government was persuaded to allocate £15,000 annually to provide grant for eleven institutions: the University Colleges at Manchester, Leeds, Bristol, Sheffield, Birmingham, Liverpool, and Nottingham, together with Newcastle, Dundee and University and King's Colleges in London. The individual grants to each were decided by an ad hoc "Committee on Grants to University Colleges". This had five members (of whom three were MPs ensuring parliamentary control). The eleven colleges received annual sums ranging from £500 to £1,800. Two conditions were attached: first, that the institutions should publish annual financial statements and second that approval for Government grants would depend on the test of academic standing.

Ad hoc committees similar to that of 1889 were appointed from time to time and by 1904, when there were 14 colleges on the list, the total grant had risen to £27,000. In that year it was doubled to £54,000 and in 1906 to £100,000. (ANNEX 2).

In 1906 the "University Colleges Committee" was appointed and made the important recommendation that the Government Allocation should be made to the committee for distribution and not direct to the colleges. This established the "arms length" relationship between government and the institutions. As well as Government funding, many colleges received payments for teacher training which by 1912 almost equalled the exchequer grants of £1 50,000.

The financial provision however remained uncertain. The universities and colleges had made great contributions to the national effort during the war but their finances were still unstable. The then President of the Board of Education (H.A.L. Fisher, a former Vice-Chancellor of Sheffield) called a meeting of all institutions of university rank in England, Scotland, and Wales. The outcome was the establishment in 1919 of the first University Grants Committee. The terms of reference of the Committee were –*"To advise the government on the application of grants made by parliament towards ......university education and to assist in ....planning the development of the universities ....to ensure that they are adequate to national needs"*. So planning was part of its functions and national needs were the touchstone.

The funds received by the University Grants Committee from the Treasury were nearly £1 million in 1919 and by 1926 this had increased to £1.5 million.(ANNEX 2) The Committee adopted principles of major importance. First, that grants to the colleges should be block grants. This respected the financial autonomy and responsibility of the institutions. Earmarking for specific purposes was kept to a minimum and used only in special circumstances. Second, the committee decided to visit the institutions. These visits (which became known as UGC Visitations) gave the Committee direct and personal knowledge of the work and needs of individual institutions and they remained a strong factor in relations between the Committee and the universities and colleges. Lastly the Committee maintained the principle that grants should depend on academic standards and quality.

At the turn of the century the early university colleges had been chartered as independent universities with power to award their own degrees (ANNEX3) - Manchester in 1880; Birmingham 1900; Liverpool 1903; Leeds 1904; Sheffield 1905; and Bristol 1909. The College at Reading was unsuccessful in first applying for a Royal Charter in 1920 but a second petition in 1925 was successful, and the charter was officially granted on 17 March 1926 the college becoming the University of Reading. After the First World War late-comers were university colleges at Leicester and Hull. In Leicester from about 1912 support for a Leicester University grew. The war intervened but in 1918 a fund was opened by two local doctors for the purpose. Then on 11 March 1919 the City Council accepted a bequest of £5,000 for the purpose of setting up a University conditional on the Council acting within a year of the testator's death. A public meeting on 2 April produced a unanimous vote to go ahead. Following the meeting Mr Fielding Johnson, a Leicester worsted manufacturer and a man of considerable wealth, wrote to the Mayor on 4 April stating his intention to gift to Leicester Council the old Asylum Building with its estate of 37 acres which he had purchased for £40,000 with a view to its use for the new University College and for resiting the Boys' and Girls' Grammar Schools. In 1921 the college began with appointments of its first Registrar and first Principal. Hull was the last university college established before the Second World War through the generosity of T.R.Ferens, a leading industrialist, who in 1925 donated £250,000 to endow it. The Corporation gave a site and £150,000 towards building and equipment, and promised an annual grant.

By 1938-9 the Treasury grant to the UGC was £2 million; in 1945 it was raised to £5.5 million and in 1946 to £9 million. (ANNEX 2).

After the second world-war the universities and colleges had enrolled a large intake of students returning from the armed forces. Most had graduated by 1952 but there was a steady growth in the size of sixth forms and the increased awards from local and national authorities meant that more qualified pupils were financially able to enter university. Also the increased number of births in the last years of the war and up to 1947 would later create still further pressure on university places. The country was becoming alive to university education about the time it became alive to national health needs. The 1950s and 1960s stand out as an astonishing period of almost feverish activity and as the starting point for political involvement in higher education. Nottingham had been chartered in 1948 and the first "new" post-war university was Keele in Staffordshire founded by the UGC and chartered in 1949. In the 1950's the remaining four university colleges were chartered as universities – Southampton 1952, Hull 1954, Exeter 1955, and Leicester 1957. (ANNEX 3)

In February 1956 the government issued a White Paper on Technical Education Cmd. 9703. This classified the Local Authority-financed further education colleges in England and Wales as either Local, Area, Regional Colleges or Colleges of Advanced Technology (CAT). Ten Colleges were selected as CATs to concentrate on full-time courses at an advanced level leading to a Diploma in Technology and External London degrees and to develop research. (ANNEX 4). They became autonomous institutions with an independent governing body on which LEAS, universities, and industry were represented.

From 1962 they were financed by direct grants from the Ministry. They responded to their new status with energy and initiative. Research was fostered and developed and new buildings and halls of residence erected. The number of their full-time students reached 10,000 in 1962, 14,000 in 1964, and 16,000 in 1965. By 1964 some 4,000 students had gained the Diploma of Technology which was accepted by universities as academically equivalent to a good honours degree. Sandwich courses were their great contribution with alternating periods of practical experience in industry with work in college on academic studies. This required close working relations with industry. Judging that technological training would be incomplete and of less value to students without them many colleges developed courses in economics, sociology, management, and administration.

The increasing number of students at universities and CATs focused attention on the cost of financing their tuition. In 1958 Government appointed the Anderson Committee to consider "Grants to Students". The Committee's report in 1960 seemed more concerned with the social effects of funding decisions than the cost effects. The Committee thought Higher Education should not be a free service with Government meeting all tuition costs because it would create the expectation "*that university education is a kind of national service to which all good students must aspire*". Free provision would also lead to questions about how individuals are chosen for university entrance and to public pressure on institutions to explain the rejection of unsuccessful candidates. Such public concern over selection for university entrance would lead to Increasing reliance "*on examination marks only, (claimed to be 'objective'), to the exclusion of personal judgments of character and other relevant factors."* Payment of all fees from public funds would also lead to *"a centralised bureaucratic control of calculation and payment of the appropriate grant to each institution"* which the Committee was not prepared to support.

In 1960 the UGC exercised its duty *"to assist in the preparation and execution of plans for the development of the universities as may be required to ensure that they are adequate to national needs"* and recommended that seven new universities be established in England to meet the growing and continuing demand for university places. This was accepted by Government. Universities could only be started by Government which provided 70% of recurrent expenditure and 90% of capital expenditure for existing universities. It was obvious that local resources were not capable of launching a new university. A university town had a certain prestige and over twenty locations submitted to the UGC claims of suitability to receive a university. In selecting the final seven locations the UGC applied three criteria: the level and strength of local financial support, the suitability of the offered site for the new institution, and the capacity of the local community to provide accommodation for students. The chosen were Brighton, Canterbury, Coventry, Colchester, Lancaster, Norwich and York. (ANNEX 5). The seven universities were chartered between 1961 and 1965. For each university an 'academic planning board' was set up to select and recommend the appointment of a vice-chancellor, key members of the academic staff and the chief administrative officers and to advise and guide the institution in its early years. Forward-looking people from other universities were attracted by the challenge of shaping a university from scratch and when appointed to the staff they brought a fresh outlook to the place of a university in a changing world. They had to take decisions on their broad academic policy and strategy; and plan the development of the site for academic and residential accommodation.

Although the UGC had provided for the future it was time for political perspectives. In 1961 the Prime Minister, Harold Macmillan, set up a Committee on Higher Education under the chairmanship of the economist Lord (Lionel) Robbins to consider the future national need for higher education and how to provide for it. The Committee's Report published in 1963 calculated that a total of 328,000 full-time places would be needed in higher education as a whole by 1967-8 of which 197,000 should be in institutions of university status; and that the figures for 1973-74 should be 392,000 for all higher education and 218,000 in universities and for 1980 560,000 and 350,000 respectively. In light of the statistical evidence the government accepted this as a basis for planning up to 1973-74. (ANNEX 6). To deal with that expansion the report recommended establishing six new universities; enlarging existing universities with many increasing their student numbers to 8,000 or 10,000 each; and giving university status to the Colleges of Advanced Technology. Since the UGC had just set up seven universities the Government did not accept the recommendation for six more.

The Committee considered that the recognition of Technology as the basis of economic development should be demonstrated by the establishment of institutions of higher technological education and research. They noted that there was too little in the country compared to such institutions abroad as Massachusetts Institute of Technology and the

Technical High Schools at Delft and Zurich. Their Report recommended that five Special Institutions for Scientific and Technological Education devoted to high level teaching and research should be developed as soon as possible (Para 383) of which one should be "*developed from one of the existing Colleges of Advanced Technology*" (Para 386 & Recommendation 54). For the other CATs it was recommended that they "*should in general be designated as technological universities with power to award both first and higher degrees*" (Para 392 & Recommendation 56). Ten Technological Universities would have transformed public perception of the importance of the technologies and of the professional opportunities they offered. Unfortunately this historic opportunity was undermined by the Committee itself. In Recommendation 392 they wrote "*We recommend that in future these colleges should in general become technological universities, and that this should be recognised in their title* ***if they so wish.***" So when they became universities most CATS dropped the word 'technological' from their title and soon became indistinguishable from the generality and were perceived as just one of thirty-five. (ANNEX 7). The exception was Loughborough which became the Loughborough University of Technology. In 1996 after Loughborough Training College (renamed Loughborough College of Education) and the Arts College were absorbed into the university it dropped "of Technology" from its title, becoming "Loughborough University". This failure to establish a distinct sector of technological higher education would be replicated in the later translation of Polytechnics into universities.

Leaving aside London only five universities in England in 1964 had more than 5,000 students and the average for the rest was 2,200.(ANNEX 8). So rapid an increase from the 126,000 students in Great Britain in 1964-65 to 197,000 in 1967-68 and 218,000 in 1974-73 was viewed in some university circles with mingled incredulity and alarm but the universities accepted the situation and expanded as quickly as the flow of government finance for buildings allowed.

From April 1965 the CATs were placed on the UGC list giving funding parity with universities. Academic salaries were brought into line with those in universities to give parity in staff recruitment and an academic advisory committee was set up for each to help in drafting of a charter and the making of key appointments.

The Treasury allocation to the UGC reached £74.5 million in 1963-64 and then represented 71.3% of the total income of universities. (ANNEX 9) The funding for 1964-65 was £89.6 million. With the CATs included in the UGC list the budget rose to £116.9 million in 1965-66. In addition, from 1947 grants for capital expenditure and permanent equipment were a feature of provision made for universities and over £266 million had been spent for this by the end of 1965. In 1960 16 universities in England were listed as grant-aided institutions. By 1966 there were 33 (ANNEX 10).

In 1964 a Labour Government under Harold Wilson was elected. Anthony Crosland was appointed Secretary of State for Education & Science and on 27 April 1965, in a speech at Woolwich Polytechnic he made a major statement on higher education. *"In Britain"* he said *"the system (for higher education) must be based on the twin traditions which have created our present higher education institutions." "These"* he continued *" are broadly of two kinds. On the one hand we have what has come to be called the autonomous sector represented by the universities in whose ranks, of course, I now include the colleges of advanced technology. On the other hand we have the public sector represented by the leading technical colleges and the colleges of education. The Government accepts this dual system as being fundamentally the right one, with each sector making its own distinctive contribution to the whole. We infinitely prefer it to the alternative concept of a unitary system, hierarchically arranged on the "ladder" principle, with the universities at the top and the other institutions down below. Such a system would be characterized by a continuous rat race to reach the first or university division, a constant pressure on those below to ape the universities above, and a certain inevitable failure to achieve the diversity in higher education which contemporary society needs."*

(That analysis has, in my view, been borne out following the abolition of the dual system by the Major government.)

A year later in May 1966 the Government published the White Paper (Cmnd.3006) "A Plan for Polytechnics and Other Colleges" listing proposed polytechnics and on 5th April 1967 the Secretary of State in a Parliamentary Statement (Administrative Memorandum 8/67) confirmed the provisional list of 28 Polytechnics in England and Wales and accepted the need for two others to be decided later. (ANNEX 11). The polytechnics were probably the last chance for a prestigious higher technical educational system for this country.

In the General Election of June 1970, the Labour Government was replaced by a Conservative. Prime Minister Edward Heath appointed Margaret Thatcher as Secretary of

Education. Her general view of students was not positive (she had been physically attacked at Enfield College of Technology); She wrote in her memoirs : "*The student protests of the time, far from being in the vanguard of progress, were phenomena of a world that was about to pass away. The universities had been expanded too quickly in the 1960s. In many cases standards had fallen and the traditional character of the universities had been lost".* However her White Paper: Education: A Framework for Expansion,(Cmnd, 5174) stated: "*The government consider higher education valuable for its contribution to the personal development of those who pursue it; at the same time they value its continued expansion as an investment in the nation's human talent in a time of rapid social change and technological developments."*

The polytechnic policy of the previous government remained unchanged. At the ceremony inaugurating the North East London Polytechnic on 10 September 1970 Mrs. Thatcher stressed *"the large and important part which she expected polytechnics to play in the expansion of higher education. They were and would remain different from universities and have a character of their own."* Her successor as Secretary of State, Norman St John Stevas, at the City of London Polytechnic in February 1973 assured the polytechnics about their future. He said: *"The polytechnics are, of course, different from the universities but they are on a par with them in the provision of higher education - this is recognised by the Government, and increasingly so by industry and young people."*

Numbers in higher education were expected to grow but the economic situation was not favourable. The UGC had warned universities in 1970: *"It seems probable that grants for*

1972-1977 will contain strong pressure to reduce unit costs". This forecast proved accurate when in December 1973 the Chancellor of the Exchequer, Anthony Barber, cut the annual increments to the UGC funding for the rest of the quinquennium by half and stated that this *"could be accommodated without detriment to the planned growth of the universities".* This cut of fifty-percent in the inflation supplement cut universities' budgets overall by ten per cent.

The leading British universities were still regarded as equal to American and as the best in Europe. But this was to change. Universities were suffering from a decline in public confidence and respect. The memory of the student disturbances of the 60s, the state of the economy, and the growth in student numbers contributed to increasing public interest in the now massive funds supporting higher education. Concerns were aired that the universities were socially exclusive. As we have seen the terms of reference of the University Grants Committee included "assisting in planning the development of the universities to ensure they are *"adequate to national needs".* So some overall central policy and direction for academic development was always accepted by the universities from the beginning. From the mid-1970s however governments increasingly began to impose more direction through detailed central planning and operational control. By 1976 the UGC acknowledged that the DES was responsible not only for overall student numbers but also for the spread between arts and sciences and undergraduates and postgraduates.

The Wilson Government, returned in 1974, maintained the policy of separate roles for the universities and the polytechnics with different funding agencies; different staff conditions and unions; and different governing structures. The polytechnics had their first and postgraduate degrees validated and awarded by the Council for National Academic Awards and were primarily teaching centres though industry sponsored projects supported much research and personal basic research of staff advancing their disciplines was also fostered.

Labour was positive about education and especially higher education but again the economic situation restricted development. Cuts of grant levels continued; the number of university students was cut by ten per cent and academic posts were frozen and building programmes cut with building of student residences virtually ended. The morale of university staff was not helped when the Houghton Committee (1974) recommended, and the government accepted, salary scales for the polytechnics, technical colleges and education colleges which in senior positions were higher than the national scale for university teachers. The AUT demanded at least parity and went to arbitration. The AUT won the case but then a government freeze limited all wage claims to £312 per year and the gap in salaries between universities and the public sector remained.

In 1976 James Callaghan became Prime Minister (1976-79) and Shirley Williams Education Secretary (1976-79). The economic situation dominated the political scene and forced the Government to seek aid from the IMF and the "Winter of Discontent" changed the Government in 1979.

In 1981 Prime Minister Margaret Thatcher appointed as Secretary of State for Education Sir Keith Joseph who believed in cutting government spending and lowering taxes. Treasury provision for the Department of Education and Science for 1980-81 was cut by 8% compared with 1979 and in July 1981 the grant provided to the UGC required institutions to make budget cuts of up to 18%. This and further cuts of five per cent in real terms over the following three years imposed severe strains on the university system with individual universities facing reductions ranging from 40% to 6% with an average of 17%. The new universities - Salford, Aston, Bradford and Keele suffered severely. Salford, the worst affected, had its budget cut 40% in three years and was advised by the UGC to lose more than 1200 student places. Most universities achieved the necessary reduction in expenditure by early retirement of staff (for which Government gave a special funding of £80m). Some three thousand academic posts were left unfilled. Academic salary increases had fallen well below the average for non-manual staff. (This was the point at which a new young accountant, member of Leicester's auditor's team, came with all seriousness to tell the Finance Officer that the University must stop trading and that the auditors could not sign the accounts!).

The universities hoped that a period of level funding (increasing in line with inflation) would follow but by 1984 it was clear that grants would be less than level and they would be expected to make up for the shortfall by increased efficiency. The 1985 Public Expenditure White Paper proposed that the UGC grant should increase at an average rate of 2.5% per year in cash terms, well below the Treasury forecast of the rate of inflation.

Keith Joseph also thought that the expansion of universities had gone too far and that students and universities had lost their way. In response the Committee of Vice-Chancellors and Principals (CVCP) and the UGC agreed that

CVCP should set up a Committee to report on the efficiency of management of universities. The terms of reference (ANNEX 12) were worked out between the Department of Education, UGC and CVCP and the Committee under the Chairmanship of Sir Alex Jarratt, Chancellor of Birmingham University, was appointed in April 1984. Although the formal terms of reference suggested the exercise was an inquiry internal to the CVCP and the UGC some saw it as a Government examination of the efficiency of management of universities. The centrality of Government (and indeed the Prime Minister's) interest was thought by some to be demonstrated by the appointment to the Committee of Sir Robin Ibbs, the Prime Minister's Adviser on Efficiency, and by the attendance at most meetings of the Committee of Mr. Ian Beesley, Head of the Efficiency Unit at the Cabinet Office who was accepted as Sir Robin's alternate. (ANNEX 13).

The Committee's Report in 1985 begins with an Introduction describing the organisation of the studies. Efficiency studies were commissioned in six universities: Edinburgh, Essex, Loughborough, Nottingham, Sheffield and University College London (Para 1.3). Each study comprised a General Study on the effectiveness of the institution's general management structure and administrative systems including the decision processes, authority and responsibility for and monitoring of the use of resources, and management information services and a separate Special Study on a specific aspect of the particular institution's structure and systems (Para 1.4). Each Study was undertaken by a member of staff of the institution designated as the Study Officer who was guaranteed independence in the work and assisted by management consultants chosen by the institution from three firms nominated by the Efficiency Committee to tender for the work at that institution (Para 1.7). All the Studies provided evidence for the Committee's main Report.

The purpose of the Committee's recommendations was stated in paragraph 2.12 of the Report: *"The crucial issue is how a university achieves the maximum value for money consonant with its objectives." "It has been a constant theme in this Report that we see a need for change throughout the university system." (Para 4.25). "An important part of any plan for change, not least when resources are limited, must be the search for value for money." (Para 4.26).* So the Report has at its centre the twin themes of Value for money and Accountability. The catch-phrase 'value for money' was the fashionable and favourite mantra of the Government. National life could have been the better if it had adopted the slogan "*money for value*" and defined the values for which it would provide.

The Report places the responsibility for the search for value for money on the "*Academic departments (which) are the key units in most universities*" (Para.3.69). They "*are the basic budgetary units*" (Para.3. 70) and as "*budget centres*" are to be "*held responsible to the planning and resources committee for what they have achieved against their budgets*" (Para 5.50). Departments are to be judged not qualitatively on academic scholarly and scientific excellence but on their resource management measured on a quantitative basis. Each department should maintain a "*profile*" of "*indicators of performance*" (Para 3.33 and ANNEX 14) - to include *"standing costs of space, utilities(telephone etc.) market share of applications, class sizes, staff workloads, graduation rates and classes of degrees"*

Accountability, the second theme of the Report, relies on monetary measurements to identify deviation of expenditure from a budget plan. *"Each budget centre should prepare an annual plan including a budget covering all the expenditures for which it is responsible. When this has been approved or amended by the planning and resources committee and Council, the centre (ie academic department) should be monitored and held fully accountable for the plan's fulfilment".* Suited to this purpose *"The profile should provide budgetary control by showing for each head of expenditure current commitment, expenditure and variance from budget."*

To deal with this budgetary responsibility the Report stresses that a professional managerial competence will be necessary. Paragraph 3.70(a) states the new perspective that management skill, rather than academic leadership, is the essential quality for heads of departments: *"(a) The headships of departments are key appointments. Ideally the individual should be both a manager and an academic leader. We take the view that it is preferable to retain the two functions in one person. In circumstances where this is impracticable, we believe the head of department must possess the requisite managerial capabilities and that he should be encouraged to delegate some part of the responsibility for academic leadership to others."* The Report relegates to a mere secondary and subordinate role the academic leadership previously regarded as paramount namely the maintenance of the highest standards in research and teaching; the encouragement and direction or influence of the research of younger staff members and advancement of their careers; presentation of the department and university at national and international professional seminars and conferences; support for publication of work of staff members even if the wait for a major book may appear to take supposedly "unproductive " years and fostering reputations of staff members and advancing their appointment to higher posts elsewhere.

As an anonymous poet wrote in 1646 of new Puritan laws
Listen to me, and you shall hear, *New fashions are devised*
You never heard the like before.
You see the world turned upside down.

The Committee's Report (Chapter 2.2) acknowledges the previously universal understanding that *"Universities in the United Kingdom are independent self-governing bodies"* but qualifies their associated freedom and self-direction as *"a large degree of constitutional autonomy".* The Report would further materially reduce that autonomy. Governments had always managed the overall policy and direction for the development of higher education by setting external parameters and financial constraints on the institutions. The Jarratt Report would propose that Government through the UGC should audit the internal management processes and skills of the universities and evaluate their professional business performance. The report recommends a business-like vertical management model for universities:- Councils asserting their responsibilities in governing their institutions (as a Board of Directors) ; recognition of the Vice-Chancellor as chief executive of the university; Heads of Departments appointed by Councils as line-managers with clear duties and responsibility for the performance of their departments. To meet the demands of this structure the Committee of Vice-chancellors and Principals should undertake responsibility for developing management skills in Vice-Chancellors, Pro-Vice-Chancellors, Deans and Heads of Departments.

The Report requires compliance from the universities. The University Grants Committee (UGC) was to monitor the implementation of the Report by each university and enforce compliance. " *Within the next twelve months, every university should prepare a programme for implementing the recommendations in this report .It would then be"* for *" the UGC to monitor the implementation of the agreed plans, and to take progress into account when allocating grants."(* Para 4.27)

The Report gives notice that the accountability of the departmental budget centre is to be extended to accountability of the institution and to inter-university comparability. "A *range of performance indicators should be developed, covering both inputs and outputs and designed for use both within individual universities and for making comparisons between institutions."* (Para 5.4)

One of the last acts of Keith Joseph as Secretary of State was to receive the Jarratt Report from the Chairmen of CVP and UGC. Kenneth Baker, his successor as Secretary of State, obtained assurances from CVCP that the Report would be implemented and from the UGC that research funds would be distributed more selectively; that tenure needed to be weakened; and that it would consider mergers of small departments. The Government then issued a press release (6 November 1986) stating that it had demanded *"real progress in the development of the policy of selectivity, the rationalisation of small departments, better financial management and improved standards of teaching."*

In return universities received a reasonable financial settlement and an increase in academic salaries.

The Jarratt Committee recommended that the UGC should monitor and enforce implementation of its Report (Para 4.27). The Committee however then questioned the 'fitness' of the UGC for its task: *"Government should commission an examination of the role, structure and staffing of the UGC."* (Para 5.1). Government acted on this by appointing the Croham Committee which reported in 1987 (Review of the University Grants Committee Cmnd.81 1987).
The Committee recommended that there ought to be greater accountability (ie government oversight) for funds provided to universities; and that the UGC be given statutory status, reduced in size and have a majority of non-academic instead of primarily academic members.

The 1988 Education Reform Act, constructed on the ostensible foundations of the Jarratt and Croham Reports, went beyond even their proposals and established a comprehensively different relationship between Universities and Government. The Act marks the boundary between a higher educational world in which society through Parliament paid and trusted the universities leaving them to carry out their social and professional duties of excellence in teaching and research responsibly and efficiently and the post-1988 world in which Government pays but increasingly does not trust the universities and through successive Secretaries of State oversees and directs them.

The Act replaced the UGC by the Universities Funding Council (UFC) and established the Polytechnics and Colleges Funding Council (PCFC). The Secretary of State appoints the chairman and fifteen members of each and a representative of the Secretary of State is entitled to attend and take part in deliberations (but not decisions) of the Councils or their committees. The Secretary of State is entitled to receive copies of any documents distributed to members of the Councils or of their committees. Universities shall give the UFC such information as it may require and Institutions funded by the PCFC shall similarly give such information, to the Secretary of State. Each of the Funding Councils shall comply with any directions given to them by the Secretary of State.

An effective Control Structure was now in place which would be developed and extended in the next two decades with threatened grant sanctions compelling universities to implement Government policy directives as recommended by Jarratt. The Act provides that the Funding Councils have power to make grants to any university or institution subject to terms and conditions as they think fit and such terms and conditions may include, in particular, conditions "*enabling the Council to require the repayment, in whole or in part, of sums paid by the Council if any condition subject to which the sums were paid is not complied with*". British universities were now clearly part of the state apparatus of education, a part of the public services. Kenneth Baker wrote in 1993: "*The academic establishment at the universities was the first professional middle class group whose practices and interests were challenged by the Thatcher Government.*" Civil servants, physicians and lawyers were to follow, although all proved tougher than the academics.

Section 202 of the 1988 Education Reform Act dealt with the issue on which Sir Keith Joseph had strong convictions (ANNEX 15). The Jarratt Committee had noted that "*The Secretary of State said he intends to legislate on tenure.*"

The Committee described *"tenure"* in terms of its adverse managerial effect as *"not allowing for dismissal on grounds of redundancy"* which it concluded *"has inhibited change and even discussion of change"*. Sir Keith had left office in 1986. Section 202 however fulfilled his intention by providing that there: *"shall be a body of Commissioners known as the University Commissioners"*, five in number appointed for three years by the Secretary of State. Section 203 defined their duty as *"securing that the statutes of each institution include (a) provision enabling the dismissal by reason of redundancy of any member of the academic staff* (appointed or promoted on or after 20th November 1987) and *(b) provision enabling an appropriate officer to dismiss any member of the academic staff for good cause"*. For this the Commissioners *"may make modifications of the statutes of any institution as they consider necessary or expedient."* The late Professor John Griffith, a socialist academic from the LSE and a consistent advocate of academic freedom, aptly compared the Act to the dissolution of the monasteries. Certainly the Act recalls Cromwell's Commissioners appointed in 1534-35 to report on the ecclesiastical estate of the monasteries and for ascertaining the quality of religious life in religious houses.

In a speech at Lancaster University in 1986 Secretary of State Kenneth Baker had proposed doubling participation in higher education over a fifteen-year period. In fact in the seven years between 1985/6 and 1992/3 the number increased by over 50%. In 1985/6 there had been 909,300 students in higher education; by 1992/3 there were 1,408,800 - an increase of 56%. While the numbers at universities remained almost stationary the numbers in polytechnics and colleges had grown.

The polytechnics had made a massive contribution. Total numbers in the polys had gone from 169,741 in 1965-6 to 454,809 in 1992-3 an increase of 167%. The largest increase was in full-time and sandwich from 31,830 to 264,260 an increase of 730%. In 1992, there were 272,400 mature students in polytechnics, 57,200 in universities. (ANNEX 16).

As they grew the leading polytechnics developed their syllabuses beyond engineering and teacher education. Law began at Manchester Polytechnic in 1966 and at others soon after. In the mid-1970's recreation and sport and leisure studies and in the 1980s Nursing, Physiotherapy and Occupational Therapy were offered as these practices allied to medicine sought to become graduate professions. By the late 1980s computing had become a major field and by the 1990s business studies in which modern languages were taught as part of the business syllabus

The Coucil for Academic Awards which validated Polytechnic degrees also approved postgraduate degrees particularly where research was supported and regarded as important as at Portsmouth.In the early eighties however the polys had taken some of the power from CNAA Under the Education Reform Act 1988, polytechnics and higher education colleges in England and Wales were no longer under local authority control, and became autonomous institutions. The Polytechnics and Colleges Funding Council (PCFC) was created and funded over 50 polytechnics and colleges previously funded by local education authorities.

In mid-1989, Kenneth Baker (1986-89) was replaced as Education Secretary by John MacGregor (1989-90), who continued the policy of support for the polytechnics because he said they had *"a track record in meeting demand"*, were dedicated to *"the learning of practical applications"* with courses *"characteristically related to the needs of industry and commerce"* and brought *"the benefits of higher education to many who would not otherwise have enjoyed them".* The number of polytechnics had remained at thirty from 1973 but in 1989 Humberside was designated; in 1990 Bournemouth; in 1991 Anglia; in 1992 West London.

The cost of higher education had become an increasing burden and central concern to Government and would remain increasingly so into the next century. The Treasury had had no control of university funding when student fees were paid by local authorities but had to increase local authorities' budgets whenever fees increased. In the 1970s the Treasury had refused to increase fees in line with inflation and replaced them by per-capita direct Treasury Grants and later Secretary of State Kenneth Baker(1986-89) introduced different per capita rates for arts, science and medical students. Student support also changed. Keith Joseph (1981-86) had not increased student maintenance grants in line with inflation; Kenneth Baker abolished social security benefits for students which had previously supplemented the maintenance grants. The Baker 1988 White Paper *Top-up Loans for Students* noted that the cost of maintenance grants had risen from £253 million in 1962/3 to £829 million in 1987 and the Education (Student Loans) Act 1990 replaced grants by loans. While loans helped the Government stabilise student maintenance and selective research grants preserved centres of research excellence, the basic funding of universities remained erratic with decline as its principal characteristic.

At the end of November 1990 Margaret Thatcher left office and John Major became Prime Minister. In her memoirs, she summarized what had been accomplished: "*By exerting financial pressure we had increased administrative efficiency and provoked overdue rationalization. Universities were developing closer links with business and becoming more entrepreneurial. Student loans (which topped up grants) had also been introduced: these would make students more discriminating about the courses they chose. Limits placed on the security of tenure enjoyed by university staff also encouraged dons to pay closer attention to satisfying the teaching requirements made of them.*" In retrospect she graciously agreed she might have been too hard on universities and admitted that some critics "*were genuinely concerned about the future autonomy and integrity of universities. I had to concede that these critics had a stronger case than I would have liked.*"

ENGLISH UNIVERSITIES 1992 – 2012
PART 2 FROM DIRECTION to CONTROL

The years of the Major government (1990 to 1997) saw a continued progressive decline in support for the universities. The amount spent on each student had declined dramatically since 1985 when, in 2000 money, it was £8,500 in the universities and £4,750 in the polytechnics, to an average in all universities - old and new in 1997 - of £4,790. The unit of public funding in 1988/9 had been 103 in universities and 75 in polytechnics. In 1990-91 it was unified at 100 in both and it declined to 76 in both by 1996-7. The student-staff ratio had dropped from 9:1 in 1980 to 17:1 in 1998. In the years 1990-1997 the proportion of children from unskilled families going to university rose from six to fourteen per cent; the proportion of children from professional families rose from fifty-five to eighty per cent. 12% of students were from overseas and their full fees were an impressive and substantial contribution to the survival of the UK universities. The brain drain, especially to the United States, continued as academic salaries, especially for outstanding academics, became in relative terms, ever more derisory. Real earnings growth between 1981 and 1992 was: for male university teachers 8.6%; for NHS nurses 29.4%; for NHS doctors 34.5%; for male primary and secondary school teachers 35.0%; for male fire officers, 39.4%. (ANNEX 17).

At the same time the Major government (1990 to 1997) undertook the most significant reshaping of higher education by the designation of the polytechnics (and some other colleges) as universities. A remarkably casual White Paper which read more like an executive summary than a serious analysis was published in 1991 (*DES, Higher Education - A New Framework Cmnd. 1541, 1991).* It stated that "*polytechnics*" was not a term easily understood and recommended that they be allowed to call themselves universities and to compete on equal terms with existing universities. In certain cases colleges of higher education, some of which had recently been "promoted", were also eligible to become universities (ANNEX 18). The appropriate legislation was passed in 1992 and established a new umbrella organisation, the Higher Education Funding Council (HEFC) to replace the Polytechnics and Colleges Funding Council and the Universities Funding Council.

The change had political advantages for Government in doubling Britain's "university" population at a stroke, attracting more foreign students whose fees were a vital element in the funding of higher education, and centralising planning and control of all teaching and research. The polytechnics had a lower funding base than universities and that would become the standard. Major himself saw the change as attacking snobbery (ANNEX 19) (John Major, The Autobiography (London 1999). However names might change the reality did not and there remains to this day a large disparity of prestige and esteem. Labour MP Brian Walden called the change "*another example of how class consciousness has decided educational policy*".

The change put Britain out of line with most of Europe, where institutions for higher technological education are common and it lost Britain the opportunity to develop institutions such as MIT and the European Technical High Schools. While the polytechnics remained there was some hope of developing them into a group of higher technological institutions equally respected as the higher academic education institutions. They could have been allowed to continue to grow in quality and prestige towards the standard set by such as the University of Manchester Institute of Science and Technology.

John Pratt (historian of the polys) later argued that "*there is a question of whether they would have been better off as first-class polytechnics than second-class universities. They gained the title of university but they lost the specialist support of the Polytechnics Funding Council and the Commission for National Academic Awards.*" (The Times Higher Education Supplement 20 September 2002). The polytechnics however welcomed their new status. Directors became Vice-chancellors, (sometimes better paid than those in the old universities) and members of the CVCP (the Committee of Vice-Chancellors and Principals) with the prestige that endowed. Principal lecturers might become professors and deans or pro-vice-chancellors. An important change for their staffs generally was being able to apply for research funds to the Research Councils on an equal basis. Some such as Oxford Brookes University with an outstanding programme in history and the University of the West of England in Bristol saw themselves as competitors with the older universities and took on the middle-class aura of the older neighbouring universities. Some clung to their original purpose as primarily centres of technical education and applied research, closely associated with local industry. These included the University of Derby, South Bank University and Southampton Institute. Some had outstanding departments, like architecture and media at the University of Westminster and aeronautical engineering at the University of Hertfordshire. Nottingham Trent ran what was regarded as the best professional training programme for lawyers. Liverpool John Moores University and Leeds Metropolitan had outstanding programmes in sports sciences. Some such as Bournemouth University had virtually no research profile and others existed at the margins of the tertiary sector - the University of North London, Thames Valley University, the University of Luton, and the University of Wolverhampton. Britain now had universities with students doing courses in media studies, tourism, and fashion and also Caribbean Studies, Beach Management and Yorkshire Studies. The University of Northumbria had an Associate Degree in Call Centre Studies (call-centres were a fast-growing part of the economy). Liverpool John Moores had a BA in pop music; Plymouth in Surf Sciences and Technology; Luton a BA in advertising. Some older universities seemed to be emulating these: at Birmingham it was possible to do a degree in Golf Management.

Simon Jenkins saw the universities as the ultimate losers in the change. "The end of the polytechnic appeared a clear victory for the university, as the monopoly supplier of higher education in Britain. Yet in my view it was not the university but the polytechnic that triumphed. The constitutional status of the British University had been shattered. In its place was Baker's concept of a work-oriented, vocational, commercial institution, run more like an externally accountable public corporation than a collegium of scholars. This concept was essentially that of a polytechnic. The local authority sector may have lost the war but it won the argument. The polytechnics had not become universities. The universities had become polytechnics."

There were, by then, sixty-eight English universities.

The numbers at university continued to grow as more families became university-conscious. It was becoming clear that the English tax system could not bear the burden of expansion at the level of the best. Late in 1995, with the universities increasingly in financial difficulties, Gillian Shephard, then Education Secretary, agreed with Labour to set up
a committee on the funding of higher education (The National Committee of Enquiry into Higher Education) to report after the impending election (which was eventually held on 1 May 1997). The Committee's terms of reference were: "*to recommend how the purposes, shape, structure, size and funding of higher education (including support for students) should develop over the next twenty years.*" The Chairman, Sir Ron Dearing had served as Chairman of the Universities Funding Council and had chaired previous committees on education. Over 14 months, 240 meetings and 380 public submissions, Dearing and his committee of academics, students, school teachers, business people and civil servants presented a comprehensive report "*Higher Education in the learning society*" in July 1997, two months after New Labour was elected to government. Dearing's report was the first national study on higher education commissioned by the government since the Robbins report of the early 1960s. The Report prompts the thought that the Committee was writing part of the Queen's Speech setting out the higher education political agenda for the New Labour government (which was elected with a massive majority). The Report dealt at length with the two elements, funding and access, which would occupy much of political and public debate in the next ten years and dominate and colour New Labour's attitude to universities for almost a decade.

In an Appendix the Committee reviewed the state of higher education. Full-time student numbers had increased by 71 per cent between 1989/90 and 1996/97. In 1996-97 2.8 million students were educated in universities and higher education colleges (including the Open University) at a total estimated cost (including student support) of £7.4 billion. One in three of young people entered higher education in 1996/97 compared with one in six in 1989/90 **though students from less affluent backgrounds continued to be under-represented.** Part-timers comprised just over a third and female students accounted for over half. Almost two thirds were mature students and their number exceeded the number of 18 to 21 year olds. The Committee considered that participation in higher education should rise from the present 32% to a national average of 45% without lowering standards or increasing drop-outs or failures.

The Committee noted that Government planned to spend around £7.6 billion (including student support) in the 1997-98 financial year and that plans *"for the next three years assume a reduction in real terms of expenditure per student of 6.5% over the two years 1998-99 and 1999-2000. This in addition to the reduction of more than 40% in the unit of funding per student over the 20 years since 1976, during which the number of students more than doubled."* The Committee estimated that for pressing short term needs an additional £350 million in 1998-1999 and £565 million in 1999-2000 were required. The Report contains 93 recommendations in all, but eight key messages: full-time undergraduates should contribute £1,000 in fees per year by loans repayable after graduation on an income-contingent basis; there should be a return to the expansion of student numbers; the world-class reputation of UK degrees must be protected; higher education should make greater use of technology; the government should increase funding for research; there should be more professionalism in university teaching and a review of pay and working practices of all staff and a stronger regional and community role for universities.

In its initial response to the Report on 23 July 1997, the Government accepted the Committee's guiding principle that the costs of higher education should be shared between those who benefit and that as graduates benefit they should share the cost. On the very day the report came out the new Secretary of State for Education (David Blunkett) accepted its central recommendation and brought in tuition fees of £1000 (a sum around a quarter of the average cost of a course) which would be paid by students. The fees were means tested, so that roughly one-third of students paid a reduced fee and only one-third the full fee. Until now all education in the United Kingdom had been free up to and including university courses. During the 1997 election there was no mention of student maintenance grants or loans or tuition fees. Now fees would be paid by students up-front with the help of interest-free loans to be repaid over the student's later professional life.

The Government later (response of 25 February 1998) explained that it had acted immediately: *"In order to avoid uncertainty, unproductive speculation, and potential dislocation of future funding".*

There was at the time little dissent to the changes proposed by his Committee. Indeed In July 1997 Sir Ron Dearing had contacted the then president of the National Union of Students, Douglas Trainer, asking him to invite leaders of student unions across the country to a meeting at

King's College London. Dearing explained to the delegates that he had recommended to the new Labour government that full-time undergraduates should pay for their university education. To his amazement, rather than arguing back, they listened for an hour and clapped as he left.

Ten years after the publication of his report Sir Ron Dearing would reflect: "*The crisis in 1996 was the result of a period of very fast growth in student numbers, financed in very substantial part by severe reductions in the unit of resource (the amount a university spends on each student for teaching); and massive decay in research infrastructure.*"

On 16 July 1998 the Government enacted the Teaching and Higher Education Act. It authorised the Secretary of State to make grants or loans to eligible students attending higher education courses and empowered the Secretary of State to set university fees. The Act by a somewhat tortuous route made it illegal for universities to decide the level of their own fees and prescribed financial penalties for any university that set fees at a level other than that prescribed by the Secretary of State. Section 22 gives the Secretary of State power by regulations to make grants to eligible students undertaking higher education and to set the "prescribed amount" of such grant available for fees. Section 26 of the Act gives the Secretary of State power to compel the Higher Education Funding Council to impose a condition on any grants made to a higher education institution requiring the institution to secure that the fees payable to it by persons undertaking courses are equal to the "prescribed amount".
Subsection 5 of Section 26 explains that "the prescribed amount" means the amount prescribed by section 22 as the maximum amount of any grant to eligible students available for

fees. An institution charging fees different from the "prescribed amount" will incur specified financial requirements which may include repayment, with or without interest, of all or part of their grant.
So New Labour made illegal the one thing - the right to charge fees at a level necessary to maintain their standards - which might have restored the universities' independence and given them the ability to compete internationally. While the provision making it illegal for them to set their own level of fees was primarily aimed at Oxford colleges, its breadth meant that all universities were then truly nationalised. The Minister for Education responsible for the terms of the Act was Tessa Blackstone MP (as she then was – later Baroness Blackstone) who was Master of Birkbeck College London until her appointment to the new Labour Government in 1997).

The 1998 Act also provided how grants or loans to students attending higher education courses should be repaid and for the recovery of amounts due for repayment. Loans for fees and maintenance would be interest-free, with repayments beginning when earnings reached £10,000 p.a. and being suspended if annual income fell below £10,000 at any time.

The Government built in safeguards to maintain its policy for increasing participation in and widening access to higher education for the least well off. Families previously eligible for a maximum maintenance grant would pay no fee at all and additional maintenance loans would ensure that no student, parent or family need be worse off than under the existing arrangements.

However it soon became clear that the fixed fees of around £1,000 per year were still not providing enough funding. Since the 1991 White Paper of John Major's

Government (*"Higher Education: A New Framework")* student numbers in higher education had increased beyond predicted levels and in total amounted to almost 1.85 million by 1998-9, an 18% increase over 1994-5. In contrast to the 18% increase in student numbers, the overall income of the higher education sector rose by only 7% in real terms. As we have seen the amount spent on each student in universities had declined since 1985 from £8,500 (1992 values) to an average in 1997 of £4,790. The student-staff ratio had dropped from 9:1 in 1980 to 18:1 in 1998 and even at the best universities there was a gradual decline in the quality of education. British universities were critically under-funded and only an increased level of fees could provide the cash injection essential to maintain their quality and esteem.

In June 2000, Lord Baker (Kenneth Baker former Secretary of State for Education) instituted a debate in the House of Lords. He judged that: *"No government of any complexion — whether Conservative, Labour or a coalition — will ever provide the funds that are properly required for higher education in our country. Our universities are, in fact, a nationalised industry. They have all the characteristics and weaknesses of a nationalised industry. It is an under-funded mass system with national salary negotiations; top down regulation of student numbers and courses; incessant bureaucratic, trivial intervention;. and under-investment in libraries, laboratories and computer rooms."*

The Russell Group Universities, (ANNEX 20) commissioned the Greenaway Report on Higher Education which calculated that to restore the unit of funding to its former level required some £3.6 billion per annum; to bring it to the OECD average £3.1 billion; to expand universities to take 50 percent of the age cohort a further £5.9 billion. The report examined the four funding possibilities which were part of the continuing higher education debate:- a graduate tax; vouchers; top-up fees; income-contingent loans; and scholarships. (David Greenaway, 'Funding Universities to Meet National and International Challenge' Nottingham University, 2000).

Top-up fees in essence meant that universities should be authorised to "top up" their fees to a level that they judged provided the funding they needed. Opponents were concerned that this would create a hierarchy of universities based on the level of fees they charged relative to their own perceived quality and lead to degrees being treated as products and to students accordingly making trade-offs between price and quality when choosing a degree. As the 2001 election approached New Labour candidates found widespread disaffection and doorstep protests on fees and opposition to further increases. These led the Party to promise that there would be no top-up fees in its second administration and that the promise would be included as an undertaking in the Party's Manifesto. The Party promised a White Paper on the future financing of higher education. There was another Labour landslide majority. The White Paper, which had originally been promised for late in 2001, was, however, constantly delayed. Everyone by then agreed that the university system was on the point of collapse but the way forward was impeded by divisions in the Labour Party and among the universities. The under-funding was plain with the tutorial and even the small seminar disappearing from the universities.

In the Singer and Friedlander Lecture at Magdalen College, Oxford on 26 September 2002 ('How to Save the

British Universities') Martin Wolf of the Financial Times made a powerful case for top-up fees but warned of two opponents:- Labour backbenchers and the English middle classes. He gave comparative statistics of higher education expenditure. (ANNEX 21). In terms of percentage of GDP: spent on higher education France, the UK and Germany ranked almost bottom; in spend on tertiary education, the UK came below France and Germany. In per-student expenditure Germany the UK and France were again bottom of the table below the OECD average.

With a commitment to a fifty per cent participation rate in higher education New Labour assumed that the failure to recruit from the economically and socially disadvantaged was the fault of the universities. Disregarded were other factors such as the frequent, though not universal, lack of parental interest in social classes IV and V, the prevailing youth culture and the weakness in state education especially in the inner cities. Of children who obtain five passes at A, B or C in GCSE only one-fifth had parents who were unskilled manual workers; two-thirds had parents whose occupations were professional or managerial. (Anthony Smith: Education, Education, Education). So-called elite institutions especially were out of favour. Evidence of elitism in the eyes of the left was that top universities which had high graduation rates were selective academically.(anathema to Old Labour) and took (on the left view) too many middle-class students from independent schools.

Of serious general concern was the experience of universities that had high drop-out ratios. But the pattern was irregular. In London, the University of North London which had 97% state school students expected a 45% drop-out rate; University College London with 60% state school intake had a 7% drop-out rate; City University with 81% state school students had a 5% dropout rate and the London School of Economics with 66% state students, a 4% drop-out rate. At ten universities at least a quarter of the students were failing to obtain any qualification: Anglia, Central Lancashire, East London, Greenwich, Huddersfield, London Guildhall, Luton, North London, Sunderland and Thames Valley.(Daily Telegraph December 2002).(ANNEX 22). At the University of Lincoln those studying tourism (admitted with average A level scores of 12 equivalent to three D's) 25% failed the first year and another 20% the second. At Liverpool John Moores 37% of those studying politics failed or dropped out. Was it that they taught badly, or took unprepared students? In the summer of 2002 the Sunday papers reported Universities of Westminster and Portsmouth both had students to read sociology who had failed all their A levels. Statistically the difference in A levels accepted for admission (ANNEX 23) was stark.(T.E.S.7 June 2002).

All these concerns aroused scepticism of the apparent obsession with the political goal of ever-increasing numbers in higher education. There was also increasing questioning of what university was for. The Anderson Report (1960 Part 1 above) had warned that it might become "a kind of National Service" and this had occurred as "university" had come to be seen as a rite of passage, at least for Middle England. The House of Lords debated higher education again in November 2002. The Labour goal of fifty per cent of all students in higher or even further education was increasingly questioned. As Baroness Warnock, a former Mistress of Girton College,

Cambridge said:- *"I believe that, one way or another, we should stop filling our universities with students who displayed no interest in academic matters at school, whose talents are more practical than theoretical, and who will not change. They may proceed to university for a variety of motives: because they are very bright; because they like the idea of student life ; or because they have been led to believe in what has been referred to as a "myth" that obtaining a degree will make them necessarily individually more employable and lead to a better salary. But too few of them have any interest in continuing to learn. They have no very clear idea of the point of what they are going to learn or what they will do with it. For many of them, their years at university will, if they stick them out, be expensive and a waste of time."* (House of Lords, 27 November 2002).

In November 2002 Secretary of State Charles Clarke issued a discussion paper (Department for Education and Skills, 20 November 2002) which addressed the purpose of universities; admitted that morale in higher education was poor with the best universities losing top faculty members and that there was a massive need for capital investment. Clarke made it clear that the rescue package to save the impoverished universities **would not come mainly from the Treasury** *"it should be clear that dependence solely upon the general taxpayer is an approach which will inevitably restrain university spending and inhibit the drive to raise standards of both teaching and research"* It was clear that the original fixed fees of around £1000 per year were not providing enough additional funding. Higher fees ("Top-up fees") were the preferred source of finance for the Prime Minister and the Education Secretary. Top-up fees with a restricted maximum would give universities more academic and financial freedom. Each university would be able to set fees at a level that would provide the funding it needed up to the maximum prescribed by Parliament. It was an effort to restore independence to a sector that had over the previous two decades become remarkably subject to central control and to put the quality of universities in place of the wishes of students and parents for "free" higher education. The proposal was, however, anathema to backbench New Labour MPs who insisted that they could not live with a price-tiered system of universities. In December 2002, the Guardian reported that, in light of Gordon Brown's opposition, and back-bench and student protests, the Prime Minister had given up on top-up fees. *"Blair signals retreat on student top-up fees"* (Guardian, 5 December 2002). But by 10 January 2003 the Guardian was reporting that Clarke would propose top-up fees of up to a maximum of £3,000, paid through loans, repayable later, coupled with the restoration of maintenance grants for the poor. On Sunday 19 January Clarke admitted on television that students could end up with debts of £21,000 at the maximum, with the average being £12,000 to £14,000. *"Graduates could be left in debt for 30 years",* (Daily Telegraph, 20 January 2003).

Clarke's Discussion Paper had the desired effect of stimulating and focusing debate in the autumn of 2002. There was general acceptance that the 136 institutions of higher education across the UK were under-funded (Annex 24). Estimates of the funding required were not less than £3 million annually, with £9 billion for deferred construction and maintenance and a further £3.6 billion if Britain wanted a fifty per cent enrolment in higher education.

The House of Commons Education and Skills Committee calculated that a fifty per cent participation rate would require 17,000 more academic staff. Meanwhile employers complained about the "dumbing down" of degrees and it was suggested that appointments at English universities were becoming mediocre (Times Higher Education Supplement April 2003). At thirty, university lecturers were earning less than MPs' secretaries and less than secondary school teachers and markedly less than teachers in the best public schools. The Guardian (21 May 2003) reported the loss of 1400 academic posts. The AUT issued a list of universities in danger of closing: Luton, South Bank, Lincoln, Greenwich, Hull, North London and Coventry. Other universities faced serious funding crises. King's College London talked of closing its famed chemistry department (Financial Times, 14 April 2003). As the old universities sought more income by taking more students, the numbers at less distinguished universities were threatened. In 2003 Leeds and Liverpool each took 2000 more students, Nottingham, 15% more; Birmingham 11%, Bristol and Manchester 9% more. Meanwhile numbers at the University of North London (now incorporated in London Metropolitan University) fell 29%. Numbers applying for higher national diplomas fell 23.4%.

In January 2003 Clarke's White Paper - The Future of Higher Education, (Cmd 5735 DES) accepted that English universities were in serious difficulties affecting both teaching and research; acknowledged that staff-student ratios had fallen from 1:10 in 1983 to 1:18 in 2000 with students having less direct contact with staff and writing fewer essays and that while research was strong *"it is declining"*, with many facilities inadequate for modern research and salaries insufficient to hold the best researchers (more than a quarter of Fellows of the Royal Society worked abroad). The amount for research was to be dramatically increased and research to be more clearly based in leading institutions. In terms of numbers, the goal was set as "*towards fifty per cent*" (Chapter 5). The Paper confirmed a six per cent increase in real terms in funding for each of the following three years. (Chapter 7 "Freedom and Funding"). Much of the expansion was to come through *"two-year work-focused foundation degrees*" many provided in further education colleges. "*We are not choosing between more plumbers and more graduates. We need both, and we need to help individuals to make sensitive and appropriate choices."*(page 58*).* That 90% of students with two A levels chose the status of a degree over a professional qualification contributed to the shortage of technicians. "*We must break this cycle of low esteem."* The goal was to make ninety per cent of young people ready for higher education or skilled employment with emphasis on persuading them to continue study beyond sixteen. Two-year foundation degrees were to be encouraged and there would be premium payments for those institutions offering associate degrees. Employers were to be encouraged to hire from two-year programmes rather than three-year ones (Chapter 3). Skills training and shortages in industry might best be met at the higher technical rather than degree level. Access loomed large (Chapter 6). It was noted that "*young people from professional backgrounds are over five times more likely to enter higher education than those from unskilled backgrounds"* and that this needed to be addressed. *"We will appoint a Higher Education Access Regulator, who will develop a framework for Access Arrangements for each institution."* The government wanted to move from judging admission by categories of "*social class, postcode and state/private school*" to "*parents' income, parents' level of education and the average results of the school or college they attended.*" The Government's commitment to quality controls in teaching was maintained and the Qualification Assurance Agency would continue to accredit university teachers with a proposed national system of external examiners by 2004/5. There were to be extra funds to reward centres of excellence in teaching.

Meanwhile in 2001, after a seven-year break, a further number of polytechnics, university colleges and higher education institutes had begun to apply for university status under the 1992 Act. By 2004/5 the title of university might be awarded to non-research institutions. In the spring of 2003 the Minister for Universities Margaret Hodge had announced the names of six new potential non-research universities expected to qualify by 2004: University College Worcester, University College Northampton, Canterbury Christ Church University College, Buckingham Chilterns University College, Liverpool Hope and the London Institution. (ANNEX 25)

The up-front standard fee of £1100 was to be abolished as of 2006, and universities given freedom to set fees up to £3000. For poorer students, the government would pay the first £1100 of fees and pay £1000 per annum in maintenance (further concessions were later offered). The White Paper pointed to increasing independence for universities: "*The Government is making an unprecedented investment in the universities and will stand by them in future spending reviews. But to be really successful, universities must be free to take responsibility for their own strategic and financial future*"

If this intent of the White Paper were carried through, it is arguable that the thrust of government policy towards universities for the last fifty years would have been noticeably reversed. In fact the change to freedom of responsibility for their own future was not immediately apparent in the wake of the White Paper and Higher Education Act 2004. Central government does not easily abandon control and increasing centralisation has been the legislative characteristic of all political parties in Government.

Following the White Paper, it became clear that the role of HEFCE was to be the Government's control and planning agency in higher education. Any residual role, inherited from the University Grants Committee, of being a buffer between universities and the state was dead. In April HEFCE produced a draft strategic planning document (HEFCE Strategic Plan 2003-08, April 2003) which saw four purposes of higher education; improving comprehensiveness, creating wealth; improving the quality of life and "*improving social cohesion, through inclusiveness and shared values*".

An Oxford University response to this noted strongly: *"The draft strategic plan marks a further step away from (HEFCE) being a body principally concerned with providing one-stream-funding to higher education, towards being a body responsible to the planning of higher education, including its overall size and shape, and future strategic development. This reflects the development of Government policy, which is* ***increasingly concerned with intervening in higher education in order to achieve political objectives.*** *There is an ambiguity running through the document as to whether higher education is part of the public sector (like, for example, the NHS), or whether HEFCE does indeed, as stated in the plan, recognise* *that universities and colleges are autonomous institutions and should decide for themselves how best to lead and manage their activities'. We note for example that the draft plan proposes key performance targets through which the Funding Council can demonstrate, in measurable terms, our progress towards the aims and objectives {in the Plan}. In many respects, therefore, the plan seems to imply that higher education is to become an intensively managed part of the public sector." (Oxford University Gazette 4 June 2003).*

In the weeks after the White Paper there was a further volume of debate on higher education conducted with even more than usual excitement and intensity. Government, HEFCE, universities, schools and the media engaged in an unstructured debate on issues of access to university and of so-called top-up fees. The idea of differential fees was vigorously attacked by the National Association of Teachers in Further and Higher Education. The universities were concerned at the proposal for an Access Regulator to monitor admissions of the poor or disadvantaged students. Sir Richard Sykes, former businessman and Rector of Imperial College, announced: "*This is social engineering at its worst. It will bring chaos into the system. They are insisting we take socially deprived kids who have not been educated properly.*" The press reported similarly. "*Plan for university regulator branded a disgrace*",(The Times,20 January 2003).: "*Degrees of access:- universities cannot make up for poorly performing schools.*". (Financial Times). Appearing before the House of Commons Education Committee Secretary Clarke said there had to be targets for working-class students. He pointed out that when Bristol accepted 9% working-class students and Wolverhampton 48% something appeared to be wrong.

He wanted less emphasis on Alevels and more emphasis on *"a range of other indicators."* *" Varsities told not just to rely on A-levels."* (Daily Telegraph, 6 March 2003). HEFCE took £265 million from teaching funds to reward universities that took more working-class and lower-achieving students. *"Universities receive extra cash to attract working classes"*, (The Times, 7 March 2003). Later Clarke admitted that universities' admissions policies were *"generally very fair"* and the Access Regulator (OFFA) the Office for Fair Access *" would not intervene in admissions policies. but suggest goals for access of students from 'poorer economic groups."* (Department for Education & Skills. Widening Participation in Higher Education 2003). *"Clarke scraps university targets for the poorest"* (The Times, 14 March 2003) *"Access regulator will not set targets"* (The Times. 31 March 2003). Universities were relieved; the left thought it was a sell-out.

The most profound contribution to the debate was the Report on Higher Education of the Select Committee on Education and Skills (Select Committee on Education and Skills, Fifth Report, HMSO, 10 July 2003) responding to the Clarke White Paper. The Committee of MPs, seven Labour, three Conservative and one Liberal Democrat, produced a unanimous Report. It was a remarkable achievement by its Chairman Barry Sheerman. He said: *" The White Paper marks a unique moment in the history of higher education and if this opportunity is missed, then we are going to regret it for a very long time."* The Report was better argued, looked more to the future, and was better balanced than the White Paper and deserves to last as a timely and crucial statement about the long-term future of higher education in England.

The Report called for greater independence and diversity for Universities coupled with an injunction to the government not *"to micro-manage what universities do".* It criticised the White Paper for being relatively short-termist, and for failing to emphasise the role of universities in the *"successful development of the potential of individuals - universities are at the very heart of the maintenance of an intellectually vigorous and civilised society".* The Report admitted that universities played an important part in economic success, but tried to put education ahead of the economy as the primary purpose of universities. The Report ended: *" a significant conclusion of the White Paper is that the Government sees universities and colleges principally as economic agents; there is very little in the document about intellectual or cultural life in higher education, or the development of the individual".*

With the cost to the Exchequer of universities reaching some £10 billion (£10,000,000,000) by 2006, the Committee shared the White Paper's view that the costs should be shared between the student, the government and the employer (through a tax on firms not undertaking significant research and development, to provide a research fund for universities). The Committee acknowledged the reality of a free-market in university applications resulting from "top-up fees" which it thought should not be £3,000 but up to £5,000, to provide a serious market. The Committee took the view that it was the absence of maintenance grants, not fees, that deterred the poor from attending universities and recommended that maintenance grants of up to £5,000 p.a. might be paid to those of poorer backgrounds in addition to waiving fees.(Para 207). Access should be left to HEFCE and the Office of Fair Access abandoned. With more than 90% of those with two A levels going to university, the Committee doubted the value of any arbitrary goal for numbers in higher education (Para. 188). The Committee calculated that a 50% participation rate would require 17,000 more academic staff and was concerned that expansion might be linked too much to the establishment of foundation degrees particularly with respect to the proposal for research-free universities.

The Committee endorsed the traditional academic argument for the essential link between research and teaching and was particularly concerned at the proposal for research-free universities. While it was inevitable that much of research would be concentrated in the international universities, there was a strong case for research funds to be distributed more broadly. Secretary Clarke was criticised for channelling research funds to fewer institutions *"We believe that the flame of research endeavour should be kept alive in all universities, and that each region of the UK should have within it a focus of the highest quality internationally competitive research"* (Para.1 88).

The Committee was especially concerned about the *"woefully low salaries"* in academic life, pointing out that the 6% increase in funding for each of the next three years was geared heavily to research and there would be no funds for real increases in salaries. The Committee suggested that, rather than spending money on centres of teaching excellence, the money should go to improve salaries. (Paras 83-85.).

The Government responded to the Select Committee (Department for Education and Skills (press release 28 July 2003) and provided a House of Commons debate in September 2003. Secretary Clarke was not about to make changes. The limit for fees was to be £3,000, the Access Regulator remained and while the Government might consider remitting fees to poorer students, there was no possibility of serious maintenance grants. The government appeared determined on the White Paper solutions arguing that UK universities required additional funding to compete internationally and that not all taxpayers, including non-graduates, should provide it. Fees were the appropriate source of funding. Opponents stressed Labour's manifesto pledge not to introduce "top-up" fees during the current Parliament and argued that allowing universities to charge different fees would put off poorer students from going to the better more expensive universities though they proposed no practical alternative solution.

At the end of 2003 parliamentary approval of top-up fees looked unlikely. The government's majority in the House of Commons stood at 161. Given the diversity of views of MPs on the issue both Government and Conservative Party agreed that the vote was too close to call. The vote would fail if 81 Labour MPs and all opposition MPs voted against. There were about 150 Labour signatories of an Early Day Motion which objected to the proposals for top up fees but predicting the size of rebellion against the government was uncertain. Both the Conservatives and Liberal Democrats opposed the plans. Prime Minister Blair having said his authority was riding on the issue would be expected to call a vote of confidence in his leadership if the government lost. In the event the Higher Education Bill was backed by 316 to 311 after days of intense canvassing by ministers and rebels. The close vote saw a major reduction in the government's usual majority of 161 in the tightest victory of Mr Blair's premiership.

MPs voting for: 316. MPs voting against: 311. Labour MPs opposed: 71. Labour abstentions: 19. Three Tories did not vote against the plans. So by 5 votes (316 FOR - 311 AGAINST) Charles Clarke's Bill became the HIGHER EDUCATION ACT 2004 receiving Royal Assent on 1 July 2004. If all Tories had opposed the plans, the government majority would have been just one.

The Act implemented the policies set out in the White Paper *The Future of Higher Education* (Cm 5735 22 January 2003) which defined the Government's position on higher education as a whole and it also created the Office for Fair Access promised in *Widening Participation in Higher Education (8 April 2003).* The Introduction describes the Act as: "*An Act to make provision about complaints by students against institutions providing higher education; to make provision about fees payable by students in higher education; to provide for the appointment of a Director of Fair Access to Higher Education; to make provision about grants and loans to students in higher or further education; to limit the jurisdiction of visitors of institutions providing higher education; and for connected purposes.*"

Part 1 provides for the Arts and Humanities Research Council which is to be established by Royal Charter for carrying out, facilitating, encouraging and supporting research and instruction in and promoting awareness of the arts and humanities.

Part 2 replaces the chartered autonomous jurisdiction of university Visitors as the final arbiter of complaints or disputes between a university and a student or former student by "*a body corporate designated by the Secretary of State to provide a scheme for the review of qualifying complaints.*"

A complaint relating to matters of academic judgment is not a qualifying complaint.

Part 3 of the Act is titled *Student fees and fair access.* Access and fees are certainly linked or welded together but their relative importance would be better expressed by the title *Fair Access and Student fees.* Fees are dependent on universities having approval for their plans for promoting Fair Access. Here is the basic nexus between university practice and policy on fair access and the fees that may be charged. Institutions are free to set their own fees up to the government specified basic amount (£1125 in 2006). To charge more a university will have to have an appropriate "plan" detailing how the institution will encourage students from poorer backgrounds to apply for entry to its courses. When an approved plan is in force fees may be higher than the basic amount but must not exceed the Government specified higher amount (£3125 for 2006 entry). Plans must define the measures the institution will take to attract students who might otherwise not consider higher education and to attract students who are members of groups which are under-represented in higher education. Plans must also provide for the monitoring by the governing body of progress in achieving these objectives. (Annex 26A – Annex 26B). The Director of Fair Access (appointed by the Secretary of State) is charged with approving university plans and required generally to promote and safeguard fair access to higher education while under Section 32 protecting academic freedom. The Director may give guidance to universities on the matters he will consider when deciding whether to approve plans and approve plans as he thinks fit. The Act provides that if an institution breaches its plan, the Director (37(1) may choose **not to renew the plan** or may direct the HEFC to impose financial sanctions, including (a) repayment, with or without interest, of the whole or any part of any grant, loan or other payment, (b)the withdrawal or reduction of any amount of the grant, loan or other payment in question that has been awarded but not yet paid, or (c)the refusal to award any other grant, loan or other payment. The Director's power not to renew the plan is the most draconian sanction. With an approved plan an institution could charge fees of £3125. Without the plan fee income would drop by two-thirds being restricted to the basic amount of £1125. The Director monitors the performance of institutions in implementing the conditions of their Approved Plans. OFFA and HEFCE jointly carry out the annual monitoring asking all institutions with an OFFA-approved Access Agreement and/or which have submitted a Widening Participation Strategic Assessment (WPSA) to submit a monitoring return. .The return is to include a report setting out progress against milestones and targets and detail the institution's: (i) additional fee income from students paying a higher fee and the number of such students; (ii) expenditure on OFFA-accountable bursaries and scholarships; (iii) number of students in receipt of an OFFA accountable bursary or scholarship; (iv) expenditure on additional outreach activities or other access measures.

Regulations provide that (a) any decision of the Director affecting a university has initial effect as a provisional decision from which (b) the university may apply for a review to a person, or panel appointed by the Secretary of State, and the Director must reconsider the provisional decision having regard to any recommendation of the person or panel.

Under Section 32(1 & 2) the Director must protect the academic freedom of universities. (Under sub-section 6) Regulations may not refer to:- (a) particular courses or to how they are taught, supervised or assessed, or (b) criteria for admission of students.

The Government had expected that the "university institutions" (as we should perhaps call them since not all were universities in the previously understood term) would charge different overall fees or varied fees for different courses. In fact all the u-institutions each submitted 'plans' (which were all approved) for charging the maximum "higher amount" £3,125 (2006 entry) each wishing to declare their status as equal to all others.

The "basic amount" and the "higher amount" are prescribed by the Secretary of State (Sub-Section 24 (6)). Section 26(2a) provides that the Secretary of State (2a) may not increase the *basic amount* nor the *higher amount* unless— (i) the increase is required to maintain its value in real terms, or (ii) the regulations have been approved by each House of Parliament, and (iii) **in case of the *higher amount* unless each House of Parliament after 1st January 2010 resolves that it should be increased to a specified amount from a specified date.** The Act's prohibition of any increase in the maximum amount before January 2010 was a gesture to the opponents of fees. Vice-Chancellors by contrast continued their assertion that the fee ceiling of £3000 fixed for at least six years (increased annually to compensate for inflation) was inadequate for their needs. The temporary prohibition of any change in the basic and higher amounts before 2010 provided an open door for further increases to be imposed by future majority governments by the "secondary legislation" of regulations passed by both Houses of Parliament. The process would be used within seven years by the succeeding Government.

In October 2004, Tony Blair announced he would not lead the party into a fourth general election but would serve a full third term. Labour won the 2005 election with a reduced parliamentary majority and reduced vote share. On 7 September 2006 Blair announced that he would step down within a year. Brown was the clear favourite to succeed Blair and on 27 June 2007 he became Prime Minister. He appointed Alistair Darling, who had been his Chief Secretary to the Treasury, as Chancellor of the Exchequer. Within a year of becoming Chancellor Darling oversaw the biggest financial storm Britain had experienced in decades.

In September 2007, for the first time since 1860, there was a run on the British bank Northern Rock. The sub-prime mortgage financial crisis in 2007 had caused a liquidity crisis in the UK banking industry and Northern Rock was unable to borrow as required by its business model. Ultimate authority for deciding on financial support for a bank in exceptional circumstances rested with the Chancellor. Darling authorised the Bank of England to lend Northern Rock funds to cover its liabilities and provided an unqualified taxpayers' guarantee of the deposits of savers in the bank in an attempt to stop the run. Northern Rock borrowed up to £20 billion from the Bank of England, and Darling was criticised for becoming sucked into a position where so much public money was tied up in a private company. He effectively saved the British economy from the brink of collapse but, given the largest post-war deficit he had created, resulting in large scale public spending cuts, he is often criticised as Chancellor.

The cuts would apply to the universities but the Department of Business Innovation and Skills in 2008-2009 focused on a long-term strategic policy for higher education and on 3 November 2009 published the Labour Government's blue-print for higher education:- ***Higher Ambitions – The future of universities in a knowledge economy.*** The Executive Summary succinctly and clearly states the key measures of that Government's strategy. It begins with the familiar government qualified acknowledgement of the principle of university autonomy: *"Our success in higher education is rooted in a commitment to* ***institutional autonomy within a framework of shared values and goals."*** *"****Free to define their own strategies for achieving core national priorities****, universities and colleges have developed new ways of contributing to our national life."* The Summary sets out policy on **access.** *" Fairer access has to remain a key part of how our world class universities see their missions." "Many universities are using contextual data to assess the aptitude and potential to succeed of those from poor backgrounds. While the Government does not interfere with admissions procedures, we believe the use of contextual data could help ensure that high-potential candidates are not missed by the system."* **wider participation:** *"The Government remains committed to the goal that at least 50% of young people should enter higher education" "We will give priority to widening participation by promoting a broader range of course models alongside the three year degree." "This will be achieved through partnerships between universities and further education colleges and by support for new local higher education centres.* **the quality of the student experience:** *"All universities should publish a standard set of information setting out what students can expect in terms of the nature and quality of their* *programme including how much direct contact there will be with academic staff and what their own study responsibilities will be."* **universities:** *"Universities have enjoyed a benign financial climate over recent years. The Government will need to direct funding more strategically if the resources provided* ***are to achieve public policy goals.*** *Universities may need to withdraw from activities in which they cannot achieve excellence in order to focus on the areas where they can."* ***"Funds will be diverted away from institutions whose courses fail to meet high standards of quality or outcome." "Excellence in teaching*** *should be recognised and rewarded alongside excellence in research," "excellence in both teaching and research is key."* **Research:-..**"*Excellence must remain the defining basis for allocating research funding." "not every institution should feel that maximising its success in the research assessment exercise is central to its mission."* **Funding** *"The burden of financing higher education's diversity of excellence will need to be more equitably shared between employers, the taxpayer, and individuals."*

Reduction of the national budget deficit and the level of Government borrowing to finance expenditure were the determining constraints on the Labour Government policy. The last Grant Letter from the Labour Secretary of State Peter Mandelson on 22 December 2009 reduced Capital Grant by £534 million and Earmarked Funding Grants by £86 million. The Recurrent Grant for Teaching was reduced by £49 million from £5076 million to £5027 million while Recurrent Grant for Research was increased by £109 million from £1509 million to £1618 million. The Secretary of State stressed "*the objectives that the Government looks to you to meet in spending the funds allocated"* are *"greater efficiency, improved collaboration and bearing down on costs combined with a commitment to protect quality and access." "we will want some shift away from full-time three year places and towards a wider variety of provision."*

At the 2010 general election the Labour Party lost 91 seats in the House of Commons the party's biggest loss of seats in a single general election since 1931. No party achieved the overall majority of 326 seats. The Liberal-Democrats (57 seats) could with Labour (258 seats) share a Government without an overall majority (315) or with the Conservatives (306 seats) share an overall majority Government (363). Negotiations between The Labour Party and the Liberal Democrats failed and Gordon Brown tendered his resignation as Prime Minister to Queen Elizabeth II and recommended that she invite the Leader of the Opposition, David Cameron, to form a government. The Conservatives and Lib-Dems agreed on a range of common policies and took office as a Coalition Government on 11 May 2010. Reduction of the national budget deficit and of the level of Government borrowing to finance expenditure were the determining constraints on Coalition Government policy as they had been for the Labour Government in its closing stages. On 24 May 2010 the Coalition Chancellor of the Exchequer announced £6.2bn of in year savings across the whole of Government.

The Department for Business Innovation and Skills like all Departments was required to achieve a budget reduction. The Higher Education Act 2004 had prescribed the level of fees universities could charge between a "basic amount" and a "higher amount" set by the Secretary of State (Sub-Section 24 (6)). It had also provided (Section 26(2a) that the Secretary of State may not increase the *basic amount* nor the *higher amount* unless—"*in case of the higher amount, each House of Parliament* **after 1st January 2010** *resolves that it should be increased to a specified amount from a specified date."* The date was fortuitous for the Coalition Department for Business Innovation and Skills. A budget reduction of Government Higher Education funding could be achieved by increasing funding through fees and in December 2010 the Coalition Secretary of State Vincent Cable announced that the Government intended to triple the level of fees increasing the basic amount to £3000 and the higher amount to £9000. Students responded by a protest march organized by the national union of students which resulted in major public disorder created by a small group of those taking part.

On 14 December 2010 the Government's legislation trebling university tuition fees passed comfortably through the House of Lords being passed by 283 votes to 215.. In the Commons the Government's majority had been 21. With those new funding arrangements from 2012 there would be a new 'regime' for HEFCE and new priorities for universities. In the Grant letters from the Department for Business Innovation and Skills to HEFCE of both the outgoing Labour and the new Coalition Governments there are **two distinctive strands** at that time. **First reductions of Grant** and **second a clear intent to direct the operations of the universities by the "control guidance" of the Department transmitted through HEFCE.**

On 20 December 2010 the Department of Business, Innovation and Skills wrote to HEFCE providing details of the allocations that the Coalition Government would make to the Council for 2011-12 and giving indicative totals for 2012-13. The Department recalled that since taking office, the Government's overriding priority has been to reduce the fiscal deficit. *"Higher Education has had to take its share of savings, but will continue to receive significant public funding with the new feature that* ***more funding will be provided directly to students, as up-front tuition loans and less will be routed to institutions as grants via the Funding Council.*** *These new arrangements coming into force from the academic year 2012/13, will contribute to eliminating the structural deficit."*

The letter confirmed a teaching budget for 2011-12 representing around a 6% reduction in teaching grant for 2011-12 against the comparable figure for 2010-11. The letter however stresses that ***"our funding reforms mean that, by 2014-15, the BIS loans outlay to HEIs for the up front costs of graduate contributions is projected to rise by some £4 billion****, from around £3 billion in 2010-11 to around £7 billion by 2014.* ***Putting together recurrent grant for Teaching and Research and the BIS loans outlay to HEIs, the aggregate effect could be that total BIS investment in HEIs in*** *England would rise from around £9 billion in 2010-11* ***to around*** ***£9.5*** *billion in 2013-14 and* ***£10 billion in 2014-15 an increase of nearly 10% in cash terms."***

The letter is principally concerned with the Coalition Government's policy for Higher Education and the priorities it was setting. The content and tone convey an intention to require and to impose changes to universities' operational attitudes and practices and to the function and operations of the HEFCE (Higher Education Funding Council for England). ***"We are setting some new directions for higher education"*** *"We will set out our overall thinking and plans for HE in more detail in a White Paper."* ***"Taken together this grant letter and the White Paper will supersede all previous directions to the Council about policy objectives.***

In particular, the White Paper will set out our intentions for the future powers and functions of the Council. For 2011-12 and 2012-13 we expect the Council will continue on its existing statutory basis."

So 2011-12 would be a year of change in which BIS wanted HEFCE to note *"a number of areas that we think are particularly important." "*Foreshadowing the forecast White Paper the areas are stated as: **Access** *"**Social mobility**, fair access and widening participation **should be a key strategic objective.*** **Teaching quality**, *"emphasis on teaching quality is fundamental to our vision for Higher Education." "built around assuring and improving the experience of the student."* **Student choice** *"to support student choice we have committed to improving the information available to prospective students, so that applicants can make well informed choices, and that **students can hold institutions to account** for the quality and cost-effectiveness of what they provide."* **Providers** *"to remain competitive as providers in the new funding environment universities will need to be responsive to the changing demands of students and employers. "**Institutions chosen by students** because they offer better quality, responsiveness and value for money **should be able to grow if necessary at the expense of those that perform less well. We expect new providers to enter the sector** provided they offer cost-effective teaching to high standards." **Research** "You should ensure that research capital is focused on maintaining excellent departments and take forward recurrent funding for research by **selectively funding on the basis of only internationally excellent** research."* **General** *"We look to the Council to continue to maximise the proportion of funds allocated to front line delivery of teaching and learning."* **Efficiency savings** *"We expect universities and* *colleges to continue to deliver efficiencies, in all elements of teaching, research and administrative activity including those from sharing services. It is essential that the sector exercises pay restraint, at a time when there is a pay freeze in place across other sectors.* **Regulated Tuition Fees** The letter ended by again announcing the **proposed increase in permitted fees** *"we have also decided that the new basic and higher amounts for students starting courses in the following academic year that is 2012/13 will be £6,000 and £9, 000."*

In February 2011 The Secretary of State for Business, Innovation and Skills (Vince Cable MP) and Minister for Universities and Science (David Willetts MP) published the **promised Higher Education White Paper 2011. The main** concern of the present paper is the effect of the White Paper reforms on the scope and range of higher education provision and on universities' professional practice and standards. It remains to present the Government intentions for change in higher education set out in the White Paper and to note the degrees of Government departmental control indicated or explicitly stated by its authors.

Chapter 1 deals wholly with the reform of financing of higher education in which the basic element was increasing chargeable fees (met by student loans) by raising the authorized "basic amount" and "higher amount" to £6000 and £9000.

Students are central to the concerns of Chapters 2 to 5 in which informed student choice; student course satisfaction; teaching quality; student career prospects; social mobility and oversight of university performance are related to the changes recommended or to be required by Government.

Chapter2 is headed "Well-informed students driving teaching

excellence". *"Better informed students will apply to places offering good value for money and excellent teaching will be every student's experience"* 2.3 *"Research by the Higher Education Policy Institute in 2007 showed marked variations between different institutions in student workload by subject."* (ANNEX 27) suggesting that "*such* variations *indicate that institutions approach teaching in very different ways."* 2.4. "***We are expecting institutions to provide information on the proportion of time spent on different learning and teaching activities.***"

2.10 "***Each university will now make available on its website information on the matters most requested by students*** *on an easily comparable basis and* ***by September 2012*** *these items called* ***the Key Information Set will be available course by course, with information about charges.*** *(*ANNEX 28) "*This will help applicants find and compare the items students consider most important.*" (Understanding the information needs of users of public information about higher education. Oakleigh Consulting and Staffordshire University 2010).

2.19 *"Better information can contribute to improved social mobility so we want schools and students to understand which GCSE and A-Level choices lead to which degree courses (and ultimately which careers, and what careers pay)"* 2.21 "*We are developing a linked longitudinal data-set of greatest value tracking typical students from school through higher education into a career."*

Chapter 3 is concerned with "*A better student experience*" and "***takes further the placing of students at the heart of the university experience by involving them in the oversight and maintenance of institutional standards".***

3.3 "*We endorse the recommendation that* ***each institution***

should have a student charter *or similar high level statement reviewed regularly by the higher education institution and students' union setting out the mutual expectations of universities and students and* ***including information on what to do if expected standards are not met.***" "*After reviewing the adoption of charters* ***we will consider whether they should be made mandatory."***

3.5 "*The National Student Survey (NSS) asks all final year undergraduate students for their views about the quality of their teaching and learning experience and overall satisfaction with the quality of the course. 3.8* ***We expect all universities to publish reports of their student evaluation surveys on their websites by 2013-14.***" 3.15-3.16. "*Institutional review which the Quality Assurance Agency (QAA) is introducing from September 2011 will have students as participants in quality assurance as well as recipients of information on outcomes and* ***each institutional review team will include a student.*** *Institutions will be encouraged to involve students in preparing action following the findings of institutional reviews.*" 3.19 "*We propose focusing Quality Assurance where it will have most impact" 6.17 "adopting a risk-based approach to quality assurance in which providers that lack a well-established track record would be expected to be subject to more QAA institutional review."*

3.27 "*One purpose of higher education is to prepare students for a rewarding career.*" 3.45. "*Enterprise societies help students develop enterprise skills and knowledge to run a business. We have challenged the HE sector to embed an Enterprise Society in all universities in England."*

Chapters 4 & 6 set out the Government intention to make the higher education sector "*a diverse, responsive and*

competitive system that can offer different types of higher education so that students can choose freely between a wide range of providers on a consistent basis." (4.6). *"We will consult on changes to the criteria for granting and renewal of degree-awarding powers at- undergraduate level and for determining which organisations are allowed to call themselves 'university' or 'university college' to make it more flexible while maintaining standards."* (4.34)
The Government introduced the first change of the criteria in November 2012. The Universities Minister, David Willetts announced that ten specialist colleges were to become universities (Annex 29) after Government lowered the threshold on student numbers needed for an institution to apply for the title from 4,000 of whom at least 3,000 study for a degree to 1,000 of whom 750 study for a degree.(Daily Telegraph 28 November 2012).
The White Paper continued *"We will also put in place appropriate sanctions, introducing the powers to suspend or remove degree-awarding powers where quality or academic standards fail.* (4.30)
"To allow students freer choice all higher education providers must be able to compete on equal terms. Current rules for controlling student numbers and awarding degrees make it difficult for colleges and alternative providers to compete with universities for students." (4.8) *"We want to introduce ways to free up student number controls, while ensuring that overall costs are managed."*(4.16. *"We are proposing to introduce a flexible "core and margin" model of student number controls Each institution will have to compete for student numbers outside its core allocation and the core will reduce every year"* (4.18). *Institutions will be free to recruit as many as they wish*

from the Margin allowing greater competition for places and giving more students the opportunity to attend their first choice institution. ***This will support expansion by providers who combine good quality with value for money and whose average charge is at or below £7,500."***

Chapter 5 deals with the contribution of higher education to social mobility which, as we have seen, featured in the last Labour BIS letter and the first Coalition BIS letter. The White Paper Executive Summary states the intention to create *"a new role for the Higher Education Funding Council for England (HEFCE)* ***making sure*** *through the Office for Fair Access (OFFA) that* ***institutions fulfil their social mobitily obligations by annual review of Access Agreements for which OFFA will be strengthened."*** *(*5.21) *"An Access Agreement approved by the independent Director of Fair Access (OFFA) is required of all institutions that intend to charge more than the basic £6,000 annual tuition charge." "****We will strengthen OFFA*** *making significantly more resources available increasing capacity up to around four times its original level* ***so that it can provide more active and energetic challenge and support to universities****"* (5.25). *"We will ask the new Director whether OFFA's current powers are right or whether clarification or extension is required which could include power to instruct an institution to spend a specific amount from its additional fee income on access or to publish OFFA's assessment that it is making insufficient progress with its Access Agreement."*

In February 2011 the Department for Business, Innovation and Skills (BIS) wrote to the Director of Fair Access setting out how the Government expected he should approach his approval and monitoring of access agreements and the exercise of his judgement. *"We want to see a shift away from assessment of inputs and processes, to a focus on clear outputs from access activities and measurable progress against appropriate measures and targets chosen by the institution and agreed with OFFA."* In other words assessing universities effectiveness in widening access by **their achievements not their aspirations – by their performance not their promises – their results not their resolves.**

The Daily Telegraph (6 September) reported the new Director of OFFA ,Professor Les Ebdon (former Vice-Chancellor of the University of Bedfordshire) as saying that the most sought-after institutions should be set "**challenging targets to create a more socially balanced student body**". He praised universities that admitted students from struggling state comprehensives with lower grade A-levels than those from high-flying schools, adding: *"Context has to be taken into account if you are going to assess potential."* The White Paper endorses this view; (5.18)."*There is evidence that for some students, exam grades alone are not the best predictor of potential to succeed at university. The Government believes that to use contextual data, for example about levels of average attainment in an applicant's school, is a valid and appropriate way for institutions to broaden access while maintaining excellence."*

(5.8*) **"We will ensure that widening participation remains a key objective of all HE institutions."** (*5.45*) "Our funding reforms will help tackle the financial barriers". (*5.28*) "A new National Scholarship Programme will begin in 2012. All higher education institutions charging over £6,000* ***will be required to participate in the Programme,*** *and* ***we will expect them to contribute additional funds from their own resources."***

(5.14.-5.15) *" We are reforming performance tables for schools introducing a measure of how well pupils do when they leave school, including information on how many progress to higher education. This 'destinations measure' will ensure that they are preparing young people for success in higher education or employment."*

6.9.*" As the balance of public investment shifts from grants to loans Government must maintain control of its financial exposure and there remains a need for a high-quality, independent lead regulator"* 6.10 *"**We believe HEFCE is the right organisation** to undertake these tasks **evolving from being primarily a funding council** to **also being the lead regulator of the higher education sector with a remit to promote the interests of students as consumers**" (Comparable to a* 'Customer Service Manager' in retail trading?).

A measure of HEFCE responsibilities is provided by the updated list of the 128 institutions it funds published by HEFCE in November 2012. (ANNEX 30). The list includes the ten new universities announced that month. (see above & Annex 29)

The White Paper states the firm intention of the BIS Department to implement the announced changes. 6.14. *" Subject to Parliamentary time, we intend to bring forward the necessary legislation to create this new regulatory framework and give HEFCE the powers it needs and to introduce the new regime from 2013-14".* 6.13 *"The new regulatory framework will comprise three broad categories: (a) as now, all institutions offering a 'recognised' degree will need to satisfy a quality threshold, administered by the QAA (Quality Assurance Agency); (b) Institutions that want their students to access student funding (loans and grants) will **need to meet further conditions:** publishing detailed information about their courses and outcomes; giving students access to dispute resolution via the OIA;(Office of Independent Adjudicator);*

complying with the quality framework; and, if they propose to charge fees above the 'basic amount' (£6,000), having an Access Agreement approved by the Director of Fair Access' "Should an institution fall to meet any of these requirements, despite having been given time to take remedial action, their access to student support finance could be suspended or stopped. We will legislate for reserve powers for HEFCE to intervene if evidence is found of widespread poor treatment of students " (4.30) "We will also put in place appropriate sanctions, introducing the power to suspend or remove degree-awarding powers where quality or academic standards fall."

The contention of this paper is that the 2004 Higher Education Act initiated a profound change from direction to control and that the Coalition letters to HEFCE and the 2011 White Paper make clear the intention to extend control.

The terms of reference of the UGC in 1952 were:- *"To enquire into the financial needs of university education in the United Kingdom and to advise the government as to the application of any grants that may be made by parliament towards meeting them' 'to assist, in consultation with the universities and other bodies concerned, such plans for the development of the universities as may be required to ensure they are fully adequate to national needs".*

Sir James Mountford wrote of those terms in his 1966 study (British Universities):

"From the point of view of the universities, there is nothing here which affects the reasonable exercise of their autonomy; so far from there being any suggestion that they may be told what they must do, they are by implication invited as responsible institutions to share in a consideration of what it is proper for them to be doing in relation to the general good of the community."

This cannot be said of English universities post-2012.

ANNEXES

ANNEX 1

UNIVERSITY FOUNDATIONS

(Date refers to foundation as college)

UNIVERSITY	Founded	Founder
Oxford - Some examples		
Balliol	1263-8)	John Balliol of Durham
Brasenose	1509	Richard Sutton of Cheshire
Nuffield	1937	Lord Nuffield (William Morris)
Wolfson	1966	Lord Wolfwon (Isaac Wolfson)
Cambridge - some examples		
Pembroke	1347	Mary St Pol,Countess of Pembroke
Gonville & Caius	1353/1557	Edmund Gonville/John Caius
Emmanuel	1584	Sir Walter Mildmay
Selwyn	1878	Selwyn Memorial Committee
Durham	1832	Cathedral Dean & Chapter
(Newcastle Kings College*)	1834/1871	College of Durham
London	1836	Group of Gentlemen
Manchester	1851	John Owens
(Manchester Coll, of Sci and Tech)	*(1902)*	
Southampton	1862	H.R.Hartley
Leeds	1874	James Kitson
Bristol	1876	Merchant Venturers
Sheffield	1879	Mark Firth
Birmingham	1880	Josiah Mason
Liverpool	1881	City Council
Nottingham	1881	Anonymous donor
Reading	1892	Town Council
Exeter	1893	City Council
Leicester	1918	Thomas Fielding Johnson
Hull	1925	T.R.Ferens
Newcastle	1963	(On separation from federal Durham)

ANNEX 2

GOVERNMENT FUNDING OF UNIVERSITY RECURRENT EXPENDITURE 1889-1946

Year	Amount	No. of Institutions
1889	£15,000	11(£500 to £1800)
1903	£27,000	14
1904	£54,000	14
1906	£100,000	(First 'university colleges committee')
1912	£300,000	(Half for teacher training)
1919	£1,000,000	(University Grants Committee)
1926	£1,500,000	
1938	£2,000,000	
1945	£5,500,000	
1946	£9,000,000	

ANNEX 3

UNIVERSITY CHARTERS

University	Name at foundation	Date opened	Date of charter
London	University College/ Kings College	1830/31	1836
Durham University		1833	1837
Manchester	Owens College	1851	1880
Birmingham	Mason Science College	1880	1900
Liverpool	University College	1882.	1903
Leeds	Yorkshire College of Science	1874	1904
Sheffield	College of Arts and Science	1879.	1905
Bristol	University College	1876	1909
Reading	University Extension College	1898	1926
Nottingham	University College	1881	1948
Keele	University	1949	1949
Southampton	Hartley Institute	1862.	1952
Exeter	Exeter Technical and University Extension College	1893	1952
Hull	University College	1925	1954
Leicester	University College	1918	1957
Newcastle	Kings College, Durham	1834/1871	1963

ANNEX 4

COLLEGES OF ADVANCED TECHNOLOGY 1956

Battersea
Birmingham
Bradford
Bristol
Brunel
Cardiff
Chelsea
Loughborough
Northampton
Salford

ANNEX 5

1960 UNIVERSITY TOWNS

Town	For
Brighton	University of Sussex
York	University of York
Norwich	University of East Anglia
Lancaster	University of Lancaster
Colchester	University of Essex
Canterbury	University of Kent at Canterbury
Coventry	University of Warwick

ANNEX 6

UNIVERSITY FULLTIME STUDENTS
ROBBINS RECOMMENDATIONS

	1958-59	1963-64
STUDENT TOTALS		
Great Britain	100,204	126,515

ROBBINS RECOMMENDATIONS:

	1967-68	197,000
Increase on 1963-64		(+58%)
	1973-74	218,000
Increase on 1963-64		(+72%)
	1980	350,000
Increase on 1963-64		(+177%)

ANNEX 7

COLLEGES OF ADVANCED TECHNOLOGY 1965

CAT	University
Battersea	Surrey
Birmingham	Aston
Bradford	Bradford
Bristol	Bath
Brunel	Brunel
Loughborough	Loughborough University of Technology
Northampton	City
Salford	Salford
Chelsea	Chelsea College of London University

UNIVERSITY FULLTIME STUDENTS 1958-1966

UNIVERSITY	1958-59	1963-64	Jan 1966
Oxford	8699	8963	**9824**
Cambridge	8844	9170	**9823**
London	20993	23955	**27378**
Durham	1398	1914	**2524**
Manchester	4626	5908	**6700**
Manchester Coll, of Sci and Tech	1487	2300	**2539**
Birmingham	3942	4982	**5715**
Liverpool	3667	5114	**5369**
Leeds	4538	6233	**6801**
Sheffield	2715	3890	**4543**
Bristol	3080	4000	**4718**
Reading	1425	1942	**2722**
Nottingham	2367	3067	**3857**
Southampton	1446	2094	**3039**
Hull	1420	2243	**3071**
Exeter	1232	1855	**2385**
Leicester	1053	1903	**2278**
Keele	689	992	**1246**
Sussex		885	**2129**
Newcastle	3556	4402	**4904**
York		220	**993**
Lancaster			**769**
East Anglia		115	**807**
Kent			**460**
Essex			**399**
Warwick			**416**
Former CAT's			
Battersea (Surrey University)			**1745**
Birmingham (Aston University)			**2059**
Bradford			**2277**
Bristol (Bath University)			**1114**
Brunel			**885**
Loughborough			**1754**
Northampton(City University)			**1834**
Salford			**2351**
(Chelsea College of London University.)			**924**
TOTALS England	77177	96147	**130352**
Wales	5851	8471	**11198**
Scotland	7176	21921	**28337**
Great Britain	100204	126539	**169887**

Robbins recommendations:

1967-68	197,000	+16%	on Jan 1966
1973-74	218,000	+11%	on 1967-68
1980	350,000	+60.5%	on 1973-74

ANNEX 9

GOVERNMENT FUNDING OF UNIVERSITY RECURRENT EXPENDITURE 1889-1965

Year	Amount	No. of Institutions
1889	£15,000	11(£1000 to £1800)
1903	£27,000	14 First 'university colleges committee
1904	£54,000	
1906	£100,000	
1912	£300,000	(Half for teacher training)
1919	£1,000,000	(University Grants Committee)
1926	£1,500,000	
1938	£2,000,000	
1945	£5,500,000	
1946	£9,000,000	
1963	£74,500,000	25
1964	£89,600,000	
1965	£116,900,000	34(CAT's included)

ANNEX 10

UNIVERSITIES IN 1960 AND IN 1966

UNIVERSITY	Charter Year
Oxford	(1167)
Cambridge	(1209)
London	1836
Durham	1832
Manchester	1880
Birmingham	1900
Liverpool	1903
Leeds	1904
Sheffield	1905
Bristol	1909
Reading	1926
Nottingham	1948
Southampton	1952
Hull	1954
Exeter	1955
Leicester	1957
Keele	1962
Sussex	1961
Newcastle	1963
York	1963
Lancaster	1964
EastAnglia	1964
Kent	1965
Essex	1965
Warwick	1965
Battersea CAT (Surrey University)	1966
Birmingham CAT (Aston University)	1966
Bradford CAT (& University)	1966
Bristol CAT (Bath University)	1966
Brunel CAT & University	1966
Loughborough CAT & University	1966
Northampton CAT (City University)	1966
Salford CAT & University	1966

(Chelsea became College of London University.)

ANNEX11

28 POLYTECHNICS (created April 1967)

Anglia
Birmingham
Bournemouth
Brighton
Bristol
Hatfield
Huddersfield
Humberside

Leeds
Leicester
Liverpool
Manchester
Middlesex
Newcastle
North East London

North London
Nottingham
Oxford
Portsmouth
Sheffield
South Bank
South West
Regent Street
then Central London
Staffordshire
Sunderland
Teesside
Thames

Two others decided later
Coventry
Kingston

ANNEX 12

STEERING COMMITTEE ON EFFICIENCY OF UNIVERSITIES 1984-85

The Committee appointed by the Committee of Vice-Chancellors and Principals in April 1984 had the following terms of reference:

to promote. and co-ordinate, in consultation with the individual institutions which it will select, a series of efficiency studies of the management of the universities concerned and to consider and report to the Committee of Vice-Chancellors and Principals and the University Grants Committee on the results with such comments and recommendations as it considers appropriate; provided that the commissioned studies will not extend to issues of academic judgment nor be concerned with the academic and educational policies, practices or methods of the universities.

ANNEX 13

STEERING COMMITTEE ON EFFICIENCY OF UNIVERSITIES

Chairman

Sir Alex Jarratt, CB, Chairman, Reed International PLC; Chancellor Birmingham University

Members

Mr. J.B. Butterworth, C.B.E., J.P., D.L., M.A., Vice-Chancellor, University of Warwick.

Sir Adrian Cadbury, M.A., Chairman, Cadbury Schweppes PLC; Chancellor of the University of Aston.

Professor F. H. Hinsley, O.B.E., M.A., F.B.A., Master of St. John's College, Cambridge.

Sir Robin Ibbs, M.A., the Prime Minister's Adviser on Efficiency.

Dr. T. L. Johnston, M.A., Ph.D., Principal and Vice-Chancellor, Heriot-Watt University.

Dr. G. Lockwood, B.Sc., D.Phil., Registrar and Secretary, Sussex University

Mr. P. I. Marshall, F.C.A., C.B.I.M., L.R.A.M., Director of Finance and Deputy Chief Executive, Plessey Company PLC.

Professor P. G. Moore, T.D., Ph.D., F.I.A., Principal, London Business School.

Professor M. H. Richmond, Sc.D., F.R.S., Vice-Chancellor, Victoria University of Manchester.

Professor Sir Peter Swinnerton-Dyer, Bt., M.A., F.R.S., Chairman University Grants Committee

Mr. S. Thomson, F.C.C.A., Director of Finance and Executive Director, Ford Motor Company

Note :*Mr. I. Beesley, M.A., Head of the Government Efficiency Unit, with the agreement of the Committee, acted as alternate to Sir Robin Ibbs on occasions when he was unable to attend meetings.

ANNEX 14

DEPARTMENTAL PROFILES
(Jarratt Report Appendix F)

Departmental profiles should provide periodic analyses of:
staff of all grades, including numbers and gross cost;

departmental maintenance, equipment and library allocations and expenditure; other standing costs of space, service utilities (telephone etc.) and general overhead;

research grants including sources, number, value and staff, equipment and materials they provide;

undergraduate numbers including applications per place and A-level scores and postgraduate student numbers distinguishing research and taught course postgraduates.

The profile should provide budgetary control by showing for each head of expenditure current commitment, expenditure and variance from budget.

It should also provide analyses of: staff/student ratios; academic/technical/clerical staff ratios; the budget centre's allocation and expenditure for each head of expenditure as a percentage of the university total; previous year and current year comparisons; and staff age distributions.

These analyses provide both inter-unit comparisons and performance indications.

ANNEX15

TENURE IN UNIVERSITY APPOINTMENTS

Tenure precluded dismissal on grounds of redundancy. Essentially, tenure gives permanent employment to retirement age with a contract that can only be terminated unilaterally "*For good cause*" namely such failure of the individual's fitness for employment as inability or unwillingness to carryout the duties of the position, grave public misconduct or moral turpitude.

The procedure for dismissal "*for good cause*" normally involved a quasi-judicial hearing respecting the natural rights of the staff member.

The legal position was not uniform across the universities but as the Jarratt Report stated *"Whatever the legal position may be, there is no doubt that a large proportion of the academic staff in universities either believed themselves to have security of tenure or act as though they have. Moreover, Senates in most universities believe that all academic staff should be treated as if they had tenure, whether or not they actually have."*

ANNEX 16

POLYTECHNIC STUDENT NUMBERS

	1965-66	1992-93	Increase
Full-time	21,788	187,668	760%
Sandwich	10,042	76,592	660%
Part-time Day	23,169	87,394	270%
Evening	21,921	27,115	25%
All students	169,741	454.809	167%

(Pratt, The Polytechnic Experiment :Buckingharn 1997).

ANNEX 17

INCREASE IN REAL EARNINGS 1981 – 1992

Fire Officers	39.4%
School teachers	35.0%
NHS Doctors	34.5%
NHS Nurses	29.4%
University teachers	8.6%

(David and Rachel Bowden: Ends Without Means.
The Conservative Stewardship of Higher Education 1979-1997
[Brighton 1997).

ANNEX 18

Two English universities founded between 1969 and 1992 were :the Open University (1969) (distance learning) and private University of Buckingham.

UNIVERSITIES POST- FURTHER AND HIGHER EDUCATION ACT 1992

The Act enabled polytechnics to become universities. 32 polytechnics did so nearly doubling the number of English universities again from 36 to 68

University	Polytechnic	Location
Anglia Ruskin	Anglia	Cambridge/Chelmsford
Birmingham City	City of Birmingham	Birmingham
Bournemouth	Bournemouth	Poole/
Brighton	Brighton	Brighton/Eastbourne
Central Lancashire	Lancashire	Preston
Coventry	Coventry	Coventry
De Montfort	Leicester	Leicester
Derby	Derbyshire HE College	Derby/Buxton
East London	East London	Stratford Newham
Greenwich	Thames	Greenwich
Hertfordshire	Hatfield	Hatfield
Huddersfield	Huddersfield	Huddersfield
Kingston	Kingston	Kingston on Thames
Leeds Metroplitan	Leeds	Leeds
Lincoln	Humberside	Moved to Lincoln 2001
Liverpool John Moores	Liverpool	Liverpool
London South Bank	South Bank	Southwark London
Manchester Metropolitan	Manchester	Manchester
Middlesex	Middlesex	London/Hendon
Northumbria	Newcastle	Newcastle upon Tyne
Nottingham Trent	Trent	Nottingham
Oxford Brookes	Oxford	Oxford
Plymouth	South West	Plymouth
Portsmouth	Portsmouth	Portsmouth
Sheffield Hallam	Sheffield City	Sheffield
Staffordshire	Staffordshire	Stafford/Lichfield
Sunderland	Teesside'	Middleesborough
Thames Valley	West London	Ealing/Slough
Westminster	Central London	London/Harrow
West of England	Bristol	Bristol'
Wolverhampton	Wolverhampton	Wolverhampton

ANNEX 19

JOHN MAJOR THE AUTOBIOGRAPHY 1999

PRIME MINISTER

Page 205

"What are our hopes?" I asked, in a speech accepting the leadership.
"Let me tell you mine. It is to build a truly open society — open because we believe that men and women should be able to go as far as their talent, ambition and effort take them. There should be no artificial barriers of background, religion or race. And I meant it. A year later I set it out once more as the general election campaign began: I want to bring into being a different kind of country, ***to bury forever old divisions in Britain between*** *North and South, blue-collar and white-collar,* ***polytechnic and university****. They're old style, old hat."*

Page 212

1991. *"In the spring I told Young Conservatives: At the top of my personal agenda is education. It is the key to opening new paths for all sorts of people — not just the most gifted — and for doing so at every stage of their lives. Not having had much education myself, I was keen on it. A theme that ran through our education policy was my innate distaste for the inverted snobbery which distorts so much of our nation's way of life. In May* ***1991*** *we launched a White Paper, one lasting impact of which was* ***to abolish the false divide between polytechnics and universities.*** *Only in Britain could it have been thought a defect to be too clever by half, I noted."*

ANNEX 20

RUSSELL GROUP OF UNIVERSITIES (16).

•

Established in 1994 to represent their interests to the Government, Parliament and other similar bodies, the members together receive two-thirds of research grant and contract funding in the United Kingdom and in 2004 accounted for 65% (over £1.8billion) of UK universities' research grant and contract income and 56% of all UK doctorates awarded.

ENGLISH MEMBERS

Birmingham University
Bristol University
Cambridge University
Imperial College London
King's College London
Leeds, University
Liverpool University
London School of Economics and Political Science
Manchester University
Newcastle University
Nottingham University
Oxford University
Sheffield University
Southampton University
University College London
Warwick University

OTHER MEMBERS
Cardiff University
University of Edinburgh
Glasgow University
Queen's University Belfast

ANNEX 21

GOVERNMENT SPEND ON HIGHER & TERTIARY EDUCATION

	Percentage of GDP	
	Higher Education	Tertiary Education
United States	2.29	
OECD* Average	1.6	
Canada	1.53	
France	1.13	1.01
United Kingdom	1.11	0.83
Germany	1.05	0.97

(Organisation for Economic Co-operation and Development: 33 Members)

	Expenditure Per Student
Switzerland	$16,563
United States	$19,802
Australia	$11,539
OECD* Average	$11,720
Germany	$9,481
United Kingdom	$9,699
France	$7,226

(Organisation for Economic Co-operation and Development: 33 Members)

(Singer &Friedlander Lecture – 22 September 2002)

ANNEX 22

DROP-OUT RATES

	State School Pupils	Drop-out Rate
University of North London	97%	45%
University College London	60%	7%
City University	81%	5%
London School of Economics	66%	4%

	A Level Score Admissions	Drop-out Rate Year 1	Year 2
University of Lincoln (Tourism)	12(3D's)	25%	20%

25% OF ENTRANTS LEAVING WITHOUT GRADUATING

- Anglia University
- Central Lancashire University
- East London University
- Greenwich University
- University of Huddersfield
- London Guildhall University
- Luton University
- North London University
- Sunderland University
- Thames Valley University

.(Daily Telegraph December 2002)

ANNEX 23

AVERAGE A LEVEL ADMISSION SCORES

1999-2000

Cambridge	29.7
Oxford	29.5
Imperial College	27.9
Bristol	26.5

1998-99

Brighton	12.0
South Bank	12.0
East London	11.7
London Guildhall	11.3
Luton	11.2
Thames	11.1

2002-03

Sunderland	2.7
Wolverhampton	2.6
Derby	2.3
Liverpool John Moores	2.3
Northumbria	2.2

Scoring count = = A-10; B-8; C-6; D-4; E-2

(Times Educational Supplement 7th June 2002)

ANNEX 24

GOVERNMENT FUNDING OF UNIVERSITY RECURRENT EXPENDITURE 1889-2001

Year	Amount	No. of UK University Institutions
1889	£15,000	11(£1000-£1800each)
1903	£27,000	14
1904	£54,000	14
1906	£100,000	First 'university colleges committee')
1912	£300,000	(Half from teacher training)
1919	£1,000,000	(University Grants Committee)
1926	£1,500,000	
1938	£2,000,000	
1945	£5,500,000	
1946	£9,000,000	
1963	£74,500,000	
1964	£89,600,000	
1965	£116,000,000	33 (CAT's included)

HEFC TOTAL GRANT AND TUITION FEES (UK)
(DES: Office for National Statistics)

Year	Amount	
1991	£2,437,000,000	107 (+29 HE colleges)
1992	£3,361,000,000	
1993	£4,908,000,000	
1994	£5,192,000,000	
1995	£5,472,000,000	
1996	£5,729,000,000	
1997	£5,693,000,000	
1998	£4,726,000,000	
1999	£5,166,000,000	
2000	£5,813,000,000	
2001	£5,628,000,000	

ANNEX 25

ADDITIONAL POST-1992 UNIVERSITIES

The **Further and Higher Education Act 1992** enabled polytechnics_to become universities. 32 had done so in 1992 nd in 2001 several more did so.

University	Date	Formerly	Location
Gloucestershire	2001	HE College	Gloucestershire
London Metropolitan	2002	Polytechnic	London
Luton(See-2006Below)	2003	Teacher Training College	Luton
Bolton	2004	Institute of HE	Bolton
Arts London	2004	London Institute	London-sites
Roehampton	2004	Institute of HE	Roehampton
Bath Spa	2005	College of HE	Bath
Canterbury Christchurch	2005	Teacher training College	Kent
Chester	2005	Diocesan(training)College	Chester
Chichester	2005	University College	Chichester
WInchester	2005	University College	Winchester
Liverpool Hope	2005	Institute of HE	Liverpool
Southampton Solent	2005	Institute of HE	Southampton
Worcester	2005	University College	Worcester
Northampton	2005	Nene HE College	Northampton
Bedfordshire	2006	University of Luton	Luton/Bedford
Edge Hill	2006	Teacher training College	Ormskirk
York St John	2006	Teacher training College	York
Buckingham New	2007	University HE College	High Wycombe
Imperial College London	2007	London College	Kensington
Campus Suffolk	2007	Five partner Colleges	Suffolk
Cumbria	2007	College & Institute	Carlisle

22 new universities brought total of English universities to 90.

ANNEX 26 A
IMPERIAL COLLEGE LONDON (ACCESS AGREEMENT)

1. This Access Agreement for Imperial College London is framed by our admissions requirements and our commitment to widening participation. 2. The College is an international university which provides rigorous and intensive degree courses in science, engineering and medicine to produce graduates for fast-track graduate employment or postgraduate study. Most courses require A-level passes in physics or physical sciences and in at least one mathematics subject and students must be well-qualified on entry. The average A-level score for 2004 entry was 28.5. 3. Courses are intended to benefit students of high ability, whatever their origin, religion, politics or sex in accord with our Equal Opportunities Policy. 4.HEFCE Performance Indicators show that in 2002-03 63% of our young full-time first degree entrants were from state schools; an increase of 9% since 1997-98. The proportion of full-time first degree entrants from low participation neighbourhoods, as defined by Government, has increased from 5% to 6.5% during this period. It is intended to continue this trend. 5. Strategy for Admissions and Widening Participation. The College places a high priority on its admissions standards and attracting high calibre students from all backgrounds. Our strategic aims are to:- Enhance the College's reputation among capable young people from a wide range of backgrounds; Continue to support applicants/students with disabilities; and Retain and support students from under-represented groups to enable them to succeed. The Bursary Scheme and our outreach programme provide a solid foundation to deliver our strategic objectives for widening access.

FEE LIMITS The College proposes to charge the maximum fee allowed of £3,000 to all Home and EU students studying undergraduate courses from 2006 entry.

BURSARIES The College has committed to set aside at least 29% of the additional fee income (estimated at £744,000 in 2006-07) for its Bursary Scheme.

The following table provides some guidance concerning the amounts involved:

HE Maintenance Grant Bursary:

Maximum at least £2,700; Mid point at least £500 ; Minimum at least £100

It is envisaged that over 30% of our undergraduate students would benefit in the first year of the Scheme. Over the past 2 years we have provided a number of new undergraduates with bursaries from the Student Opportunities Fund, financed through fundraising from alumni. These provide a maintenance grant for each year of study (up to 4 years). The College intends to continue this.

OUTREACH WORK Funding, of the order of £70,000 per annum, has been allocated to our outreach work and, in particular, to the appointment of a Director of Access, a new post, created to oversee and develop the College's outreach work of interaction with schools.

MILESTONES At least 29% of the additional income from the increased fees will support eligible students in the form of bursaries. We expect to increase the number and proportion of students from under-represented groups who apply. In 2004-05, 13.2% of applicants were from the socio-economic groups – lower supervisory and technical occupations, routine occupations and semi-routine occupations. It is intended that this should rise over the period of the Access Agreement.

INSTITUTIONAL MONITORING ARRANGEMENTS The administration of the Access Agreement will be the responsibility of the Academic Registrar reporting to monthly meetings of the College's Management Board and providing an annual Access Agreement report

ANNEX 26 B

LONDON SOUTH BANK UNIVERSITY (ACCESS AGREEMENT)

A teaching-led University, with a commitment to applied research we seek to build on our record of service "to the poor and disadvantaged of South London". It is one of the most socially inclusive in the UK. Over half of the 21,000 students in 2003-4 are from ethnic minority communities, compared (15% nationally) and 90% aged over 21 years on entry. 65% of 8,382 full-time undergraduate entrants were mature (27% nationally), 96% from state schools or colleges (88% nationally & 92% HEFCE benchmark), 44% from social classes IIIM, IV and V (29% nationally & 38% HEFCE benchmark), and 17% from higher education low participation rate neighbourhoods (14% nationally & 12% HEFCE benchmark).

2 Tuition Fees To meet our institutional obligations and to make up for shortfall in past investment we have chosen a flat-rate tuition fee of £3,000 (£3225 for 2009/10) for full-time HEFCE-funded undergraduate degree courses and for Foundation Degree, Foundation Year (Extended Degree) and HND programs offered solely by the University.

3 Outreach and Bursaries, 71% of our full-time undergraduates. coming from households with annual income less than £15,200. pay no fees.Annual bursaries will take the form of cash payments and/or support in kind. We will sustain our already very significant contribution assuming HEFCE continues its financial support.We will use a significant proportion of our additional fee income within a range of 20% to 30%. Our outreach activity is extensive and intensive. We are well above the national averages for widening participation and exceed our HEFCE benchmark. We have a Widening Participation Unit, a Community Outreach Officer and a Learning Development Centre offering pre-entry and post-entry support each devoted to advancing our widening participation strategy. Our target groups include gifted and talented students from local schools where participation in higher education is low. We provide pre-entry and post-entry learning support for approximately 9,000 students and in our outreach activity embrace around 4,000 young people annually. We run subject specific 'taster' days providing free access to University's library, computer centre, careers guidance, student cafes and bars etc. and transition programmes with current enrolment of 500 students.

4. Provision of Financial Information to Students Financial guidance is available in our website and prospectuses and we publish annually two specialist brochures offering guides to support sources and advice on financial planning and money management. From 2006-7 this information will be in the guides and prospectus and on our website 12 months ahead of the year of study and provided to prospective students through local school and colleges and our "Open Days".

6. Milestones and Monitoring Our key performance indicators will remain the location-adjusted benchmarks set by the HEFCE. And our target in the future will be to ensure that, at the very minimum, we at least meet these benchmarks and preferably, as we currently do now, exceed them.

We will monitor performance: by annual monitoring of all programmes overseen by the Quality and Standards Committee of the Academic Board; and the University's Equal Opportunities Committee which reports directly to Academic Board; and is then reported directly to Senior Management and Board of Governors; and through internal processes accompanies the monitoring return to HEFCE.

ANNEX 27

STUDENT WORKLOAD BY SUBJECT

– Highest and lowest institutional mean hours per week (average of 2006 and 2007.

Subject	Highest	Lowest
Medicine and dentistry	46.3	26.3
Subjects allied to medicine	38.3	24.6
Biological Sciences	39.9	15.0
Veterinary; Agriculture & related	41.6	23.5
Physical Sciences	45.3	19.8
Mathematics/Computer Sci	13 36.	17.1
Engineering & technology	41.2	20.8
Architecture, Bldg and Plng	41.5	26.3
Social studies	35.8	14.0
Law	4.8	18.7
Business & Admin	28.3	15.5
Mass Communications	26.8	14.7
Classics etc	39.3	14.8
Historical and Philosophy	39.5	14.0
Creative Arts & Design	34.5	17.2
Education	33.7	14.4

Higher Education Policy Institute 2007

ANNEX 28

KEY INFORMATION SET

Information for prospective HE students

The Key Information Set will enable higher education institutions to illustrate the quality of the experience that they offer. We think students should also be able to access information about the size of the different kinds of class (lecture, seminar etc) that they can expect.

Course information: a. proportion of time spent in different learning and teaching activities by year of study; b. assessment methods used by year of study; c. professional bodies that recognise course.

Student satisfaction: a..Overall satisfaction with quality of course; B.staff explain things well and make subject interesting; c.sufficient advice and support with studies; d. prompt and clarifying feedback on work; e.library resources meet needs;.f. good access IT resources.

Costs • a.accommodation costs; b. tuition charges; c. Bursaries, scholarships and other financial support.

Students' union Impact union has had on time as a student.

Employment. a. destinations (employment or further study) of students completed course; b. proportion of students in full-time 'graduate' job six months after graduating and salaries; c. salaries for subject across all institutions six months and forty months after graduating.

(Oakleigh Consulting and Staffordshire University (2010) Understanding the information needs of users of public information about higher education)

ANNEX 29

TEN NEW UNIVERSITIES 2012

The Department for Business, Innovation & Skills announced on AA November 2012 that ten smaller higher education colleges in England spanning a variety of subjects and histories including three specialist arts institutions and the Royal Agricultural College, were to become full universities. This was the largest one-off creation of universities since the then-polytechnics were awarded university status in 1992. It followed the department's reduction of the minimum student intake for a university from 4,000 to 1,000.

Arts University College at Bournemouth in Poole
Bishop Grosseteste University College
Lincoln's Harper Adams University College in Shropshire
Leeds Trinity University College
Newman University College, Birmingham
Norwich University College of the Arts
Royal Agricultural College
University College Birmingham
University College Falmouth and
University College Plymouth St Mark and St John.

The Universities Minister David Willetts in a statement said. "*It is right to remove the barriers preventing high-quality, higher education providers like these calling themselves universities simply because of their size. This will enable more people to realise their aspiration of going to a university.*"

ANNEX 30

128 HIGHER EDUCATION INSTITUTIONS FUNDED BY HEFCE (15 NOVEMBER 2012)

Anglia Ruskin University
Aston University
University of Bath
Bath Spa University
University of Bedfordshire
Birkbeck, University of London*
University of Birmingham
University College Birmingham
Birmingham City University
Bishop Grosseteste University
University of Bolton
The Arts University Bournemouth
Bournemouth University
University of Bradford
University of Brighton
University of Bristol
Brunel University
Buckinghamshire New University
University of Cambridge
Institute of Cancer Research*
Canterbury Christ Church University
University of Central Lancashire
University of Chester
University of Chichester
City University, London
Conservatoire for Dance and Drama
Courtauld Institute of Art*
Coventry University
Cranfield University
University for the Creative Arts
University of Cumbria
De Montfort University
University of Derby
Durham University
University of East Anglia
University of East London
Edge Hill University
Institute of Education*
University of Essex
University of Exeter
Falmouth University
University of Gloucestershire
Goldsmiths, University of London
University of Greenwich
Guildhall School of Music & Drama
Harper Adams University
University of Hertfordshire
Heythrop College, University of London*
University of Huddersfield
University of Hull
Imperial College London
Keele University
University of Kent
Kings College London
Kingston University
Lancaster University
University of Leeds
Leeds College of Art
Leeds Metropolitan University
Leeds Trinity University
University of Leicester
University of Lincoln
University of Liverpool
Liverpool Hope University
Liverpool Institute for Performing Arts
Liverpool John Moores University
University of London
University of the Arts, London

Continued next page

ANNEX 30 (Continued)

London Business School
London School of Economics and Political Science*
London School of Hygieneand Tropical Medicine*
London Metropolitan University
London South Bank University
Loughborough University
University of Manchester
Manchester Metropolitan University
Middlesex University,
Newcastle University
Newman University College
University of Northampton
Northumbria University
Norwich University of the Arts
University of Nottingham
Nottingham Trent University
The Open University
University of Oxford
Oxford Brookes University
University of Plymouth
University College Plymouth Marjon
University of Portsmouth
Queen Mary, University of London*
Ravensbourne
University of Reading
Roehampton University
Rose Bruford College
Royal Academy of Music
Royal Agricultural College
Royal Central School of Speech and Drama*
Royal College of Art
Royal College of Music
Royal Holloway, University of London
Royal Northern College of Music
Royal Veterinary College
St George's, University of London*
St Mary's University College
University of Salford
University of Sheffield
Sheffield Hallam University
SOAS, University of London
University of Southampton
Southampton Solent University
Staffordshire University
University of Sunderland
University of Surrey
University of Sussex
Teesside University
Trinity Laban Conservatoire of Music and Dance
UCL
University of Warwick
University of the West of England, Bristol
University of West London
University of Westminster
University of Winchester
University of Wolverhampton
University of Worcester
Writtle College
University of York
York St John University

Michael Baatz held appointments at the universities of Edinburgh and Birmingham until 1963 when he was appointed Secretary to the Collegiate Council of College Principals at the University of London becoming Academic Registrar of the University in 1966. In 1973 he was appointed Registrar and Secretary of the University of Leicester retiring in 1983.

Illustrations courtesy of
Universities of Leicester, London and Sheffield

Cover illustrations
Front cover Senate House University of London
Back cover Fielding Johnson Building
University of Leicester